LOVE YOUR LOCAL MISSIONARY

edited by

Martin Goldsmith

with contributions from
Elizabeth Goldsmith
John Wallis
Anne Townsend
Stanley Davies

Illustrations by Taffy

MARC EUROPE
STL BOOKS
EVANGELICAL MISSIONARY ALLIANCE

STL Books are published by Send The Light (Operation Mobilisation), PO Box 48, Bromley, Kent, England.

The Evangelical Missionary Alliance is a fellowship of evangelical missionary societies, agencies and training colleges that are committed to world mission. Its aims are to encourage cooperation and provide coordination between member societies and colleges, and to assist local churches to fulfil their role in world mission. The EMA offices are at Whitefield House, 186 Kennington Park Road, London SE11 4BT.

MARC Europe is an integral part of World Vision, an international Christian humanitarian organisation. MARC's object is to assist Christian leaders with factual information, surveys, management skills, strategic planning and other tools for evangelism. We also publish and distribute related books on mission, church growth, management, spiritual maturity and other topics.

British Library Cataloguing in Publication Data

Goldsmith, Martin
   Love your local missionary.
   1. Missions
   I. Title
   266   BV2063

   ISBN 0-9508396-6-3 (MARC)
   ISBN 0-9502968-3-X (EMA)
   ISBN 0-903843-92-7 (STL)

Contents

Prayers Matter So Much

Elizabeth Goldsmith

'Listen to this beautiful letter,' Martin called out to me. I had taken the post upstairs for him to read in bed, as for some time now Martin had been troubled with an uncomfortable tightness in the chest, coupled with a frightening inability to draw a deep breath. He often felt worse in the evening; so if his heavy preaching and teaching load allowed it I would bring him breakfast in bed.

I hurried up the outside staircase of our little two-roomed house in North Sumatra, waving a good morning to our neighbour who was busily grating coconuts outside her back door.

'This letter from Mrs Gilkes is amazing,' Martin continued, handing the airletter to me to read. Mrs. Gilkes was the elderly house-bound widow with whom I had lodged just before going to Missionary Training College.

'I have been praying for you so much,' she wrote. 'And as I lay in bed, lifting you up to God, I felt he was telling me that something was the matter with one or other of you. I could not be clear what it was; but I felt God was saying that I should ask him for a Christian doctor to be sent to you in case you need him – and that he should have the right medicines.'

I sat down in astonishment on the wooden box which served as our bed-side table. 'We've never mentioned in any letter that you're not well, have we?' I gasped. 'Isn't that fantastic that God should have led her to pray like that!' Maybe there was some drug which could help Martin, and to have a Christian doctor near at hand would be marvellous.

That was exactly what happened. Within a short time a Christian doctor was posted to our market town of Kabanjahe up on the mountain plateau, north of Lake Toba. His skill and carefully transported medicines brought Martin the relief he needed. The doctor had told the government that he was willing to go to a more remote assignment, and we felt sure that Mrs. Gilkes' prayers played a part in his being assigned to our town.

But what encouraged us most was that here was a prayer partner who not only used our letters to help her to pray more intelligently, but cared enough to take time to listen to what God was saying. This was the sort of partnership in prayer from our friends at home for which we longed.

On arrival among the Karo Bataks of Indonesia we had found ourselves immersed in a growing spiritual awakening.[1] Opportunities for ministry were so many we told our Mission there would be work for ten couples in the area, not just one. We had no time to convey all the details of what was taking place in our letters, and so longed for friends at home to have a sensitivity to God and a quickened imagination which would fill in the gaps for themselves.

Sometimes this brought its surprises:

'I never pray for *you*, you know,' Martin was greeted by one of his old college friends on our first leave. The warmth of welcome in the strong grip of this ex-boxer's hands and the smile on his face contradicted strongly what he was saying.

'Oh really,' murmured Martin weakly, wondering where to go from there.

'Yes, it's your widowed mother I pray for,' the friend went on. 'I've noticed so often that it's the parents of missionaries who often have a hard time. And quite frequently someone doing a vital job has to come home because of their parents. So I just pray for your mother.'

As Martin expressed his gratitude he realised how appropriate this prayer was. Some of our anxieties about our parents could not be elaborated in our prayer letter, since they themselves received these letters. What an encouragement it was to know someone was really concerned about them.

Martin had been sent out by an Anglican church which had never commissioned a missionary before. Because of this, the church as a whole had some difficulty in knowing how to support him. My church sent out regular monthly newsletters, which I joyfully pounced on, as they kept me in touch with happenings back home. But his church was

[1] See *God Can Be Trusted*, Elizabeth Goldsmith (STL Books/Kingsway)

not developed sufficiently to produce a newsletter. The backing he received came mainly from individuals, who took time to write and to share.

Both approaches were a help. My church gave regularly to my support and I knew I was frequently remembered in the central prayer meeting; but only a handful of individuals wrote to me. Perhaps this was because I had only been a member there nine months between university and Bible college, and so had not forged many deep friendships. Martin had been in his church for years and many of his friends wrote regularly. This brought tremendous strength to us, to be recipients of their sustained love and concern all the time we were overseas. It meant that when we returned home there was little catching up to do, the bonds of friendship being as close as ever.

One of his friends took great delight in keeping us informed on a variety of topical subjects. By the time he had given us the latest ecclesiastical gossip (which bishop had been moved where, or who had been appointed to a certain living) and how the various members of the royal family had been occupied recently, and what the latest cricket scores were – we felt we had skimmed through our own edition of the *Tatler*! Some of it did not interest me particularly; but we appreciated this friend taking the trouble to keep us up-to-date. And when we returned to the UK after four years and realised how rapidly things had changed, we appreciated this thoughtful touch all the more.

There were times when we could have wished for more help, noticeably when we came home on leave. Together with our first child we spent a month initially with Martin's mother and then with my parents. But Andrew was very unsettled from all the travelling and the drastic change in climate. And we were very inexperienced parents and found it a strain living with in-laws, even though they did their best to make it as easy as possible for us. Our Mission had a home we could rent and I stayed there for some months with Andrew, while Martin travelled on deputation tours. But I knew no one in the village, shopping was difficult and there was not much spiritual fellowship. I felt desperately lonely, and without even a telephone I seemed just as far away from my relations as ever I had been in Sumatra. If our church could have helped us to find some suitable local accommodation it would have greatly eased my unhappiness.

There were others besides our home churches who made a vital contribution to our work. Each year a small gift of about five pounds arrived from a Baptist church in Sussex. This was worth considerably more in those days, but it was the fact of it coming so faithfully and yet being a comparatively small amount which touched us. Martin had spoken at this church before sailing for Singapore. Five years later when re-visiting them he met the lady who so regularly sent the money. She taught the eight-year-olds in the Sunday School. Setting herself the goal of helping these children understand what missionary work involved, she decided each week to tell them one item from our newsletter. It only took a few minutes out of the class time and she always asked one of the children to pray for us. But over the year with her they built up a detailed picture of what we were doing, and any voluntary gifts from them were passed on to us. As we reflected on the strategic value of what she was doing, we realised that all the children would at some time be 'eight-year-olds' and so would pass through her hands. Also, how helpful it could have been if each class were linked in this way with a missionary from a different country. By the end of their Sunday School days the children would have gained an extensive knowledge of overseas mission.

Martin and I have been very grateful over the years to those individuals who have shown us love and support in our service for God overseas. But we realise that those with an interest in missionary work are the exception rather than the normal. We have become increasingly aware that this is because world-wide mission is not central to the teaching of most churches. This is why we feel it important, not only in preaching and teaching, but also in our books, to emphasise the world-wide perspective of the Bible. Every biblical Christian needs to face up to the challenge of God's universal love which extends to all nations. We need to align ourselves with God's purposes for the whole world.

The Missionary Abroad

John Wallis

A recent prayer letter ended, 'I still miss you madly – or am I mad enough to miss you?'!

Absence makes the heart grow fonder. And so it is when one of the church's most loved sons or daughters (or couples) is called by the Lord to go overseas. One part of the body is separated from the rest, and it is painful. But the body of Christ can and should stay together, specially that part of it in the local church. There is no surer or quicker way of drawing out a practical involvement in God's work overseas than to send a member out from a local congregation to extend that congregation's ministry further afield.

Seen this way, the missionary's work overseas is part of our work. He is our representative for the Lord Jesus in the extension of God's Kingdom. He is both an ambassador for Christ and also for the local church that he has left behind. There is no sense that he has left the congregation or said goodbye. It is more a matter of au revoir. He will be back soon and in what shape or with what success depends largely on the response of the local church.

The departure of a missionary for overseas work should be a growth point for the congregation. Sadly it is often viewed as a setback because a much-loved leader is to serve elsewhere. Thoughts of the privilege being given to the local congregation fail to be taken on board. Likewise expectation about the Lord's ability to raise up fresh leadership is low. If however we see the ministry both overseas and at home as one, we will rejoice in the new thing that the Lord is doing in the congregation. For, after all, it is he who calls, separating some for a special task he has for them.

At the farewell service there are many who promise to write, keep in touch and care. It is surprising how quickly the letters tail off, either because promises were made out of the emotion of the occasion or because the expected reply is slow in coming. Missionaries usually have a large correspondence. Just like us, some are poor correspondents and we need to be patient. But, obviously, keeping in touch is vital for both parties. Friendships, after all, are not static. They need to be fostered. The physical distance that now separates us needs to be compensated for in a practical and constructive way. Love will gladly accept the need for regular correspondence. It is often the chatty letters that help most although there will be occasions for offering advice. But hold back criticisms, realising that it is easy to get only one side of the story.

We also need to interpret what we are reading from a missionary, particularly in the early days. There are often many adjustments and new stresses. The missionary needs to feel the security of writing to friends and to be able to let off steam and blow his top. While it is undoubtedly true that some missionaries have an immediate love for the people they serve, others have arrived overseas finding within themselves a dislike for the local people that is only conquered by a deep sense of God's calling. Little by little, the missionary learns the secret of allowing Christ to love people through him.

With the proliferation of international dialling facilities today it is worth saving some money for putting through a call on special days such as birthdays or wedding anniversaries. But beware of using the telephone to try and sort out problems. That can often lead to greater frustrations.

We all know how much it helps to hear the voice of a loved one. It is readily appreciated by one church in north

London which had a regular exchange of tapes with a missionary every fortnight for four years. When the missionary returned she was not a stranger, not even to the new members who had joined the church since she had left the country. Even if you are not able to afford the luxury of a member of the congregation visiting your missionary (together with a ciné camera if possible) make sure that you have a recent photograph at the back of the church so that others keep pace with the unavoidable effects of *anno domini*.

The presentation of your missionary on the noticeboard at the back of the church is extremely important. If a photograph is dog-eared and out of date, naturally people will think this is an unimportant side of the church's life. It doesn't do very much either for the self image of the missionary, let alone the image you are trying to create of your representative overseas and the work that he or she is doing. Those skilled in graphics in the congregation should be invited to keep the noticeboard fresh and contemporary.

Little Things Count

It has been well said that love is the giving impulse. Genuine love has a fertile imagination for expressing itself. Some of the best expressions are the simple ones and not necessarily expensive. The way to the heart of a Dutch missionary may be a little liquorice! But think twice before sending a Scottish missionary a haggis for Hogmanay (unless it's going to the frozen North).

Missionary ladies always used to be classified as the 'Brogues and Tweeds' sort. Today most people are fashion conscious and it is not only the women who enjoy receiving a fashion magazine! While most missionaries are fully abreast of what is happening in Britain today, thanks to the BBC World Service, they still enjoy a good read about life

back home, supplied for example by the *Weekly Guardian*. By these various simple ways love for those separated from us by many thousands of miles is communicated.

Sometimes a piece of simple equipment can make the quality of life considerably better. The regular supply of water filters to a couple in Malaysia dispensed with the daily chore of boiling water. The water filters were either unobtainable or grossly expensive locally. When Paul wrote his thank-you letter to the Philippian Christians he said it was not so much the gift but what lay behind it that counted. An expression of oneness in the task to which the missionary has been called is also expressive of our commitment to the basic task of making Christ known among the nations. The recipient at the other end is as thrilled, as

Paul was, as much with the expression of love for Christ as with the size of the gift. If the gift can be conveyed personally by a representative of the congregation the blessing is even richer. The dividend for the church of another enthusiast for that particular work is obvious. More about visits to the missionary later.

Keeping Body and Soul Together

Missionaries are or should be committed to a simple life-style. It's quite clear in Jesus's instructions to the seventy that what he was looking for was a simple life-style (Luke 10). Since only fifteen per cent of world population enjoys seventy-five per cent of the world's goodies, many missionaries are serving in countries where failure to adopt a simple life-style can be a definite stumbling block to the preaching of the Gospel. The importance of being satisfied with having a roof over one's head, food and clothing, is great, but even that costs quite a lot in some parts of the world today. Food may be cheaper in some countries, other services are not.

The word 'love' has a hollow ring if it is not prepared to look at the hard facts of mission costs. Members of 'established' churches are particularly prone to an unbusinesslike approach to finance, especially when it comes to the support of the ministry. Thanks to the endowments of former generations they have enjoyed ministry on the cheap. The fact that these endowment funds are now running out is a great blessing to many churches, helping them to face squarely the responsibility of calling a man into 'full-time' service.

To be willing to wave missionaries farewell, without giving serious thought to their support, is highly inconsistent. If we are unaware of the costs then missionary societies are acutely aware of them. You have only to write to obtain a clear account of the figures. In today's economy, if we have a family serving overseas then we are thinking in terms of £10,000 per year, give or take a little either way. This is a sizable proportion of the church budget. Experience has proved that those fellowships which give a high priority to supporting those who have gone overseas see the blessing of God on the general level of giving in the church. It seems that the more you give away the more you receive. That should not surprise us. The Lord Jesus said, 'Give, and it will be given to you.' Some churches give more than fifty per cent of their income away to overseas or missionary work. If that is not the case in your own local congregation, then the basic tithe of a tenth of all income might be a good target for the first year. Resources do vary, however, and if we play our part then the Lord plays his in providing for missionaries from other sources. Most today have more than one supporting congregation.

Some churches have a discretionary fund to meet the inevitable emergencies that arise for those overseas. A sick relative at home, a child away at boarding school running into emotional problems, or a training conference that would be particularly helpful in terms of academic in-service training, are just some of the unforeseen things that crop up. Any family likes to set aside finances for emergencies. The church is a family, and should act accordingly.

If, however, the full support is not available, or for some reason there are not funds on hand to meet an emergency, we need not fear. There is, in fact, a blessing to missionaries in times of shortage. Cast freshly upon God, they prove his utter reliability. One missionary with no money for food was under severe pressure from her Chinese house help who quietly yet painfully mocked her trust in God. One morning at breakfast time she came to announce that the cupboard was bare. It was eight o'clock and breakfast was normally taken at eight-thirty. The missionary in faith and trust ordered the table to be laid. In the following half-hour what followed can only be described as miracle upon miracle, as one person after another arrived at the house, so that by the time breakfast was served there was bread and eggs and coffee in sufficient quantity to provide many more breakfasts.[1]

God's extraordinary provision, however, should not make us careless about his normal way of providing for those overseas. We need to be as businesslike as possible in this responsibility. The advantages of giving under Deed of Covenant are familiar, but the fact that you can do that for a large single donation, such as the provision of an air fare, is less commonly known. A thoughtful and considerate response to the financial needs of those overseas is more loving than the more erratic emotional response that characterises much of our giving. The Treasurer therefore in a local congregation carries a heavy responsibility. Sometimes his services can be stretched also to other practical matters such as looking into the care of a missionary's home that has been leased to others, or helping with private financial matters.

Prayer as Work

In our very affluent and prosperous society one of the commodities that is less willingly given to the Lord is that of time. Some of us find it easier to give money than time. Material prosperity increases the number of potential activities, particularly leisure pursuits, but all these splendid and pleasurable things, however, have an unfortunate way of consuming a great deal of time. While material prosperity should increase personal freedom, often the reverse is true. While in a sense we have more time for praying, we find it

[1] *To a Different Drum*, Pauline Hamilton, OMF Books.

harder to make space to engage in the business of prayer. The economies effected in a materialistic society are quickly swallowed up by taking on other responsibilities, so the situation arises where everybody in the congregation is too busy. Thus we rob ourselves of the highest activity of man, namely prayer, not to speak of the deeply satisfying and refreshing experience of communion with God.

At the same time we are reducing the effectiveness of our friends overseas. Although we are aware of the tyranny of the urgent over-ruling the important, we allow wrong priorities to reign. But if we understand prayer properly then no activity is more an expression of our love for Christ and for others than intercession. Discipline is required both in private and corporate prayer.

There are a number of useful helps to that end. The greatest intercessors for others have always kept a detailed prayer list. As the Spirit of God prompts and gives specific concern for prayer, so the name is noted. Without that we are moved to pray simply by the latest news we receive or situation we meet. Daily prayer for those on our prayer lists can be imaginative and creative even if the news is sparse. One praying woman was sufficiently in touch with the Lord to send to a family serving in East Asia further instalments of 'miracle money' under the prompting of the Holy Spirit. These gifts were often remarkably on target. A large dental bill received in the morning was met by the afternoon mail containing notification of a fresh batch of 'miracle money'.

If such tangible things are on target, how much more the Spirit-led prayer of those at home? Does not such prayer account for that sudden uplift out of depression or worry, or the resolving of some particular problem in the mission-ary's work? Indeed, sometimes it can be more crucial than that. During the Japanese occupation of mainland China a bachelor missionary was comforting his sister missionary, who for weeks had been under house arrest. Now they

21

were being marched onto the public square to face a firing squad. It was difficult to understand what crime had actually been committed but the ultimate test of faith was now upon them. The order to load had been given, but just at that crucial point a more senior-ranking Japanese officer came onto the square to interrupt the proceedings. He proved to be extremely annoyed with the officer in charge of the firing squad and equally apologetic to the poor unfortunate missionaries. After profuse apologies they were given freedom to roam the town and their house arrest was at an end.

When the missionary recounted this remarkable story in Australia some months later, a lady in the meeting withdrew and hurried to her home. There she consulted her diary and then returned to the meeting place. At the end of the evening she stood to address another lady with whom she had a close friendship. She reminded her of the day on which they had met in the street, when she had shared a deep sense of burden and concern for this very missionary. The two of them had withdrawn to the privacy of her home and interceded on their knees before the Lord. When the time difference was checked it was discovered that at the precise moment the two sisters in Australia were in prayer, the two missionaries were facing the firing squad in China thousands of miles away.

This is not an isolated story. In recent years, while one missionary was visiting in the southern city of Pusan, Korea, his wife remained four hundred miles north in Seoul. He had taken their wee son for the excitement of a journey, and the two of them were lying in the guest room of a long-standing Korean friend's house. The weather was somewhat chilly and in order to be hospitable the host had put on the *yun-tan* fire to heat the floor. This is an ancient method of heating, whereby the hot gases pass under the floors along flues and out of a long chimney at the far end of the building.

During the night a drama took place. The wife awoke in Seoul with pains in her stomach. Being pregnant she drew the obvious conclusion that an early arrival was to take place. Somewhat apprehensive about obtaining a taxi during curfew hours, she turned to the Lord in prayer. At that very moment all thoughts concerning her own safety passed away to be replaced by a deep concern for her husband and her son. At the same time in the house many miles away down south the little boy was waking up with pains in his stomach! The evening supper having been somewhat lavish, the conclusion was drawn that something had been eaten requiring a quick discharge. However this was not the case. The pain having passed, the two lay down again unaware of the fact that they were breathing in deadly carbon monoxide fumes.

In God's mercy the boy woke again, and this time when his father stood up he immediately collapsed, making sufficient noise to arouse the total household. It was quickly realised that the whole house was full of carbon monoxide. Since it took nearly five hours to recover in some measure from the experience, one could only conclude that the Lord had intervened through the prayers of a concerned wife hundreds of miles away. Prayer is a mystery, but it is stories like these, drawing back the curtain for a moment on God's ways of working, that make it both a worthwhile and exciting enterprise – in some cases the difference between life and death.

When it comes to praying for missionaries it is a mistake to reserve such intercession for the peripheral groups. Clearly the more intimate support in a large church with a number of missionaries is possible only through the smaller groupings. But if prayer for missionaries is not brought into the main body of the worship time as well, a wrong sense of priority will be given to the congregation. Just as it is important to keep the biblical emphasis on mission central to our teaching programme, so likewise with our prayer programme. The interest among the congregation will naturally vary, but intelligent and sustained prayer should be sought on behalf of all.

Sharing in prayer groups or cells set up by missionary societies should be encouraged, as should attendance at prayer conferences, which provide a depth of understanding for our praying that is not normally available at the local church level. Conferences are expensive today and the local church should consider sponsoring some members to attend on behalf of the congregation.

For day-to-day praying most missionary societies produce a prayer calendar. This can be referred to when the family meets for prayer together, usually after supper. Alternatively it can be used as an aid for prayer during daily times of quiet and devotion. A prayer calendar is often included in the missionary magazine. It used to be standard practice that, just as some Bible reading aid was necessary for personal devotion, so reading a missionary magazine was a part of our commitment to Christ's work overseas. Both the inroads of universalism – the belief that in the end all men will be saved from judgement and find their way to heaven – and the fear of being thought bigoted in a multi-racial society have eroded the urgency of many Christians for rescuing those that are lost without Christ. Carelessness over the need to warn the careless about impending judgement, and to provide the answer for those who are acutely aware of their shortcomings and sin, has tended to create the kind of climate whereby interest in missionary work is 'good for those who enjoy that kind of thing', but not necessarily required of all. It is surprising how many people find the whole prospect of praying for missionaries dull and without challenge, simply because they have given little thought concerning the implications of the Gospel they have received, and have not taken the few practical steps necessary to make it both interesting and relevant.

As soon as we see that prayer is not a matter of praying for the work but part of that very work, we shall see that our part at home is as important as the work being done overseas. That great pray-er and intercessor J. O. Fraser, working among the Lisu tribe on the Chinese/Burma border many years ago, wrote to his praying friends assuring them of his conviction that if they ceased their work of prayer he would necessarily have to cease his work of evangelism among the Lisu. He saw little point in continuing without the prayer backing of Christians at home.

The Unfinished Task

Dr Ralph Winter of the US Center for World Mission in Pasadena has forcibly reminded us of the unfinished task, and of how many peoples remain 'unreached'. One of the most telling statistics that he produces is that only seven per cent of our total missionary task force is reaching out in pioneer evangelism. The rest in various ways is helping the national churches. While it is true that there is a church now in most countries of the world, talk of the national churches must not blind us to the fact that the task is still largely unfinished. In some countries the church is tiny and, while without doubt the missionary spirit is the pioneer or frontier spirit, we must not neglect the 'unfinished' peoples where missionaries have been working for many years with small results.

Nevertheless, one longs to see more of that spirit of the apostle Paul when he wrote that it was his ambition to preach Christ where he had never been made known before. His plans always reached far beyond 'all the care of the churches which was upon him daily'. In a similar sense Dr

Ralph Winter has helped to create again that pioneering spirit which was such a mark of the missionary expansion following the great nineteenth-century revivals.

To focus world need an annual missionary festival in the local church can be an enormous help. Some churches run a ten-day programme taking in two weekends at either end of the event. This can be coupled with a self-denial week and a fresh look at missionary giving. If your church hasn't reached such dizzy heights then start small with a missionary weekend. The chief objects are to educate and to challenge: to educate concerning that part of the mission field for which your church has responsibility and to challenge others to consider a career as a full-time missionary.

Every available resource should be used. Because of the high number of overseas students in our country it is sometimes possible to have a national Christian present. If there is a national church leader in the country at the time, the impact of his presence and presentation is considerable. We begin to perceive the depth of spiritual power and strength of Christian leadership that exists in other countries. We too easily assume that the leadership of the catholic (universal) church will remain in European or Western hands. The truth is that leadership in the future may be more plentiful in Africa, Latin America or Asia.

Missionary societies will have some resources to share. Material for mounting an exhibition in church together with some good audio visual aids can be borrowed. The missionary meeting used to have greater appeal than it does today, partly due to the fact that we are more familiar with the world, living as we do in what Marshall McLuhan has called 'the global village'. Our multi-racial society makes stories of Bongo Bongo land and its people 'old hat'. TV travel programmes have taken away the novelty such meetings used to enjoy, and put real pressure on Christian

organisations to produce high quality video cassettes or audio visual aids. There are few Christian films of sufficiently good quality, but groups like International Films[2] are willing to give advice. Missionary meetings have received a bad press, especially among young people, sometimes justifiably so. Imaginative planning is required to gain people's attention. As the proverb has it, 'Where there is no vision the people perish.'

[2] International Films, 253 Shaftesbury Avenue, London WC2H 8EL.

The Bible is quite clear about the motivation for mission, but there is also the human story. If the story of the expansion of the Church in the book of Acts is thrilling, so are some stories of the present day expansion of the Church around the world. Equally an account of the need in different parts of the world can be challenging. While the need in itself does not constitute a call to missionary work, it can certainly bring across the challenge as to our willingness to go. Was it not the meeting with a man from Macedonia in the market place at Troas and some account of circumstances across the seas that led to Paul's well-known Macedonian call?

Focussing on some significant event in the target country is also biblical and helpful. What happens in the political and economic history of a country directly affects Christian work, and such events therefore have their part to play in raising interest. The Thai government's determination to tighten up on smuggling of heroin into the country, leading to the imprisonment of Rita Nightingale and her subsequent release from the Lad Yao Prison in Bangkok, due to a royal pardon, is an obvious starter for interesting people in God's work in Thailand.

Your missionary weekend will benefit by having a special project. When it was the International Year for the Handicapped one church provided artificial limbs for leprosy patients. They were already deeply involved with leprosy clinics in the country concerned and this was a helpful way of focussing attention on that work as well as sending a love gift that was much needed.

The opportunities afforded today by missionary societies for young people to have a short-term programme overseas gives some exposure to cross-cultural evangelism and is also an opportunity for gaining the immediate involvement of young people. As the result of such experiences, particularly with training organisations like Operation Mobilisation, many have discovered a call to lifelong service overseas. When one such young person left for her target country, Japan, the young people at the church set about raising her air fare for the return journey. Their creative approach to the task was to organise an art auction. Members of the congregation were encouraged to donate works of art, pottery, jewellery for auction and at the end of the evening, after a lot of fun, half the return fare had been raised. Many of those same people put in generous bids in the spirit of the occasion. One might well prefer straightforward glad and sacrificial giving, but sponsored walks and such occasions have their own part to play in getting young people involved.

But above all, the missionary weekend is the occasion in the year for informing the congregation as accurately as possible about all the missionaries supported by the church. It can be helpful to produce a brochure with photographs of those overseas together with a little synopsis concerning their work.

World Church Sunday or whatever it might be called is a good opportunity for involving the total congregation in prayer. The Sunday by Sunday mention of those serving overseas is helpful but not enough. Time needs to be taken during the worship to inform the congregation of the latest news, followed by intelligent prayer. Where the strategic nature of prayer is understood this is readily accepted. There are some excellent books today that can help. *Born for Battle* by Arthur Mathews (OMF Books) has helped thousands of people understand the principles of spiritual warfare and prayer. *Mountain Rain*, the updated biography of J. O. Fraser by Eileen Crossman (OMF Books), has similarly helped people to understand what is meant by the prayer of faith. The missionary weekend is a key opportunity for helping people to start reading missionary biographies. Such biographies perhaps do more than any other books to teach the principles of Christian work and to challenge the quality of our spiritual life.

The way in which God has answered prayer for individuals in a multitude of situations can be immensely stimulating and encouraging. It is for that reason that answers to prayer need to be reported to the congregation. There is nothing worse for killing off vital prayer for missionary work than failure to report answers to prayer. If missionaries are on leave it is helpful to include an interview with them during the service, drawing them out particularly by way of testimony to answered prayer. It must become clear to all that nothing happens apart from prayer. Since God has so chosen to link his activity in the world to the prayers of his people, that link must be understood. The understanding must not be a dry theological truth but a thrilling concept of being workers together with the Lord in the extension of his kingdom.

Mission and Outreach

For people who have newly come to Christ and have made the discovery of salvation in him, there is a strong fascination about the ways others have come to find Christ. The stories of the ways this has happened in other cultures and in different lands is of immediate interest. Missionary weekends can be opportunities for outreach not only in the sense of increasing the number of people interested in missionary work but of using the stories of how people have found Christ overseas evangelistically.

This means that it is appropriate to organise the widest kind of programme. Schools will often open their doors to missionaries from an educational point of view. The local library can often be persuaded to purchase missionary books and even mount an exhibition on a particular country if they are approached in time. If there is a local market in the town it is possible sometimes to arrange a stall which similarly presents a country of particular interest, at which cottage industry products such as those promoted by both Traidcraft and Tearcraft can be sold. Coffee parties, fork suppers or missionary breakfasts have all been used to good effect.

Since missionary work is the most important task of the church, involving its most public witness, a missionary weekend surely is an occasion for a very public presentation of the work of the church. It is a pity that more is not made of missionary weekends. They have often been instrumental in others finding Christ and recognising why the church exists at all. The church exists that the manifold wisdom of God might be known through it. Part of that wisdom is God's glorious plan to bring together a people for his praise and worship drawn from every nation. There is no other society in the world that enjoys such close harmony in

relationships between peoples of vastly different cultures and backgrounds.

Missionary Society and Local Church Relationships

The most appropriate time, apart from the farewell service for a new worker, for welcoming representatives from the missionary society is over the special emphasis weekend. Too often missionary society representatives come and go, having preached at morning and evening service and done little else. There is much more that they can offer. Missionary societies see themselves as the servants of local churches. The presence of the representative should be an occasion for calling together the Missionary Council or Committee for a time of discussion. There needs to be a time to share the needs of the work and the situation facing the worker. Misunderstandings can be cleared away on such occasions and any tension that might exist between the local church and the society be resolved.

It is after all a delicate relationship. After years of going it alone, thanks to the response from local churches, missionary societies are now realising the importance of closer relationships with supporting churches. For too long the task of giving a sense of responsibility for overseas work has been left to the societies. In the past, local churches have been quite content to see members join a society and then feel that their work was ended rather than just beginning. The imbalance has been redressed and the relationship between societies and local churches is very much better. It is clear from the Bible that the local church commissions new workers to go to the mission field, but the missionary society is probably in a better position to deploy that worker and find the best opening for him. If a local church minister has been involved in the selection process he probably appreciates this readily.

The missionary for his part must report back progress to the local church, since he depends on it for prayer and support for his ministry. Many missionaries have had great help in doing this when a couple in the congregation has offered to take care of the production and distribution of their prayer letter. Here again those with artistic and graphic skills can help to transform a prayer letter into a most presentable piece of communication which helps to keep the vision for the work bright and overcome lethargy in prayer and support. Decisions concerning his service overseas however are best made at the point of action rather than back home.

This means that a missionary has responsibilities in a number of directions. He is under the authority of the mission overseas, and in many cases is also answerable to the local national church. It is understandable that in recent years the local church at home has desired to have more say in the direction and ministry of their worker. Some church leaders find it hard to grasp the fact that however much they try it is difficult to get hold of the whole picture concerning a missionary situation, making judgements from the home end sometimes partial or even inadvisable. One couple received just the message they were looking for when they received advice from the home church to fly home, needing no further excuse to get out of a difficult situation. If they had stayed they would have matured spiritually and ultimately have been more useful. Over the years missionaries learn to balance these different responsibilities but in the last analysis they are responsible to the mission agency that has provided the opportunity for their ministry. Those who dislike such third parties are often the first to appreciate in an emergency the resources and skills which a mission agency possesses when the kind of help required is just not to be found on the ground.

It would be unusual if a local church did not have a pastoral concern for their missionary. That however should not override nor conflict with the pastoral care of the mission agency or national church. It is at times of crisis that the different roles of the parties involved become clear.

When it was discovered that one missionary family, because of the serious illness of the wife, should leave the country quickly, the different ministries of the body of Christ sprang into action. While the missionary society saw to the practical details of an exit/re-entry permit, the necessary flight home and notifying the home base, national Christians came to the home to pray with the couple, assist with packing and arrange for local travel to the airport. The home base for its part informed the local church of the situation and details of travel arrangements, and hospital-isation. The local church welcomed the family at the airport, and took them to a house that had been specially prepared for them. The wife was immediately admitted to hospital and support for her husband and children arranged, especially a baby sitter during visiting hours. Thus a crisis was averted and the blessing of belonging to the body of Christ experienced.

Likewise it is a relief to have the support of a society if a crisis arises at home. The missionary needs to be contacted quickly and here again there is real advantage in going through the missionary society. It is sometimes not appreci-ated how traumatic it can be for those overseas to have bad news from home if it is relayed directly to the individual, rather than routed through the mission leadership. Distance has a knack of distorting facts, and it is easy to get the whole situation out of proportion. With the ease of travel today and the ready availability of funds, some missionaries have returned home to find that they need never have come, had they only been better informed of the situation.

It is also easy for those at home to jump to the wrong conclusions concerning the situation overseas. If one relied on the media alone it would be easy to gain the impression that in Northern Ireland the troubles amount to civil war. The truth is that a small number of people are involved and for most of the time life proceeds normally. When therefore there is revolution in a country or demonstrations it would be wrong to conclude that the missionary from your church is in immediate danger. He may be. But more often than not the danger arises when the situation has not hit the news headlines. Missionaries in Indonesia came under considerable pressure at the time of elections when extremist elements began pounding on their door and demonstrating outside their home. News of this never reached the media and the incident was over before it was possible to communicate to those at home. Mission leaders on the ground are much better able to judge the danger, sometimes making a decision to withdraw from an area when those back at home cannot see any reason for doing so.

A similar situation can easily arise when a missionary is not welcomed back to his job overseas. It is difficult for a church to understand why 'our missionary' should not prove acceptable. There are usually many reasons why it may be wiser for a missionary to stay at home. These are shared as fully and frankly as possible with the local church. More often than not the reason lies in the area of inter-personal relationships – a lack of ability to get on with other people. This might be a relationship with someone in the national church, or with fellow members of the mission. How important then at the beginning is the involvement of the pastor with the Council of the missionary society in the decision to recommend a missionary for overseas service. While great care is paid to ensure that only those called and properly equipped go overseas, there can be mistakes and people do run into trouble. If a decision is made to withdraw from the mission then the worker can suffer a real bereavement which requires sympathetic understanding. In the difficult employment situation too there is need for practical help in accepting readjustment and finding remunerative employment. In other cases, where leaving the mission is not necessary, a period at home may be needed either for retraining or counselling.

The local church plays a vital role in helping workers continue to serve overseas. Contrary to expectations the demands get greater as well as the cost and it is never easy for missionaries to return for another period overseas. It is of course a great privilege, but let us not be guilty of putting our missionary on a pedestal, failing to realise that he is just like one of us, needing the love of fellow Christians and their constant encouragement. Love is patient and will wait to see how the Lord trains his servant through the many ups and downs of life on the mission field. Of one thing we can be quite certain, and that is that the Lord in his faithfulness will fulfil all the purposes he had in view when first calling his servant to missionary work.

Catching the Vision

When it took seven months by slow boat to travel to China no one ever thought of visiting the missionary. Today it takes a matter of hours and the routes are familiar to hundreds of business people. Air travel has revolutionised the interaction between those at home and overseas. The modern equivalent of the apostle Paul's visitor Epaphroditus can be a great encouragment to the missionary. For the representative of the home church it can be a time of learning and catching a fresh vision for the work. Parents too find that to visit the field takes away a great number of

36

misconceptions about their children's living conditions and work. Some missionaries however never unpack (metaphorically speaking). It may therefore be better for parents to leave their visit for a two-year period before going for the first time.

One of the lovely things that the Lord has done has been to give the parents of missionaries a real vision for the work that their children are doing. As one mother put it recently: 'When my daughter went off to the mission field it was as if she was entering a Roman Catholic convent. I really felt that I had lost her. But as a result of my visit to see her overseas I have gradually come to realise what a wonderful privilege has been given to my daughter. Although it was very hard, I am glad that I let her go now. It has brought so much blessing both to her life and mine. I would never have gone overseas if it hadn't been for God's call to my daughter, and in the whole process I've learnt so much as a Christian and come to the point of rejoicing in my daughter's work. Because I was willing to let her go I have been greatly rewarded.'

It is like Jesus's word to the disciples – 'He that would hold on to his life will lose it but the person who loses his life will find it.'

Equally, where there is wholehearted involvement with those working overseas there are many rewards for those that stay at home. How we need to catch a vision of the wider blessing of God as a result of involvement in missionary work. For those who go there are of course many hardships. If however you talk to missionaries you generally find that they would not exchange their position for all the money in the world. They have discovered that the very best place to be is at the centre of God's will, for there the blessings come.

Recently I talked to one missionary lady returning for

her final term of service. 'How do you feel about going back?' I said.

'I'm as excited as I have ever been,' was the reply. 'You see, I'm not only going back to the place where I began my ministry more than twenty years ago, but the little boy I taught in Sunday School at the beginning has recently been appointed the pastor of the church that I serve. Added to that I get back in time for his marriage to a lovely Christian girl. What more could you ask!'

It is a strange thing, but both for those who go and those who support there is often a reluctance to give our all to Jesus. Once we have done that and made the commitment we discover how foolish such reluctance is. If the calling out of a people for his own glory from every tribe, nation and tongue is the Lord's great plan for our world, then to be involved in it can only mean blessing. Perhaps, after the style of arranged marriages in East Asia, if we don't feel the passion for the arrangement at the start, the more we appreciate the wisdom of others over what has been arranged, the more we will enjoy the relationship. If our love for those who have gone overseas is somewhat cool and uncommitted it is without doubt common experience that if we make a commitment the passion will quickly follow for the work that they are doing, and we shall certainly catch their vision for the glory of God in another part of the world.

The Missionary at Home

Anne Townsend

'Why is my brother trying to look as if he's nothing to do with us?' Anne puzzled, as she caught his eye across the arrivals barrier at Heathrow Airport. It was four years since she and her three children had last seen him – and now, at last, they were actually on their first furlough.

She watched her husband deftly piling all their possessions in cardboard boxes onto the baggage trolley. She smiled in memory at the lady in the Thai market who had given her a roll of brightly coloured raffia-plastic to tie the boxes tightly so that their contents would not spill across the local bus that had taken them the four-hour journey to the airport outside Bangkok.

'Thank goodness we've learned to travel how the Thai up-country people do,' she thought. 'Cardboard boxes are far easier than cases – and ours fell to pieces ages ago anyway!'

She looked proudly at her family, and liked what she saw. Their new clothes, made in the local market, really looked good. They had saved their allowances for ages so that each of them could have a new set of clothes for the journey home. Anne had collected pictures of clothes out of Western magazines, and then chose her favourites to be copied inexpensively by the seamstress in the local market.

She waved confidently at her brother, who promptly disappeared in the crowd, owning them only when they were through and merged with others. It was years later before he confessed, 'I nearly died that first time you two came home. There you were in "imitation" clothes, with all your belongings in boxes – you looked like refugees!'

That returning missionary family faced the joys and pain that are common to most – a complex reaction to the familiar that has become strangely unfamiliar. It has neatly been summed up under the term 'culture shock in reverse'.

Returning Home

No matter how well your missionary has kept up with what is happening (in his home land, in his native culture, and in his family) returning home is nearly always a shock.

The more your missionary has learned to identify with, and feel with, the culture to which God has sent him, the greater the shock of re-entry into his home culture. He will be hit at all levels of his humanity – body, mind, emotion and spirit. Your patience and understanding as he gropes his way into feeling comfortable again in a culture in which he unexpectedly finds himself an alien, will be more important than you can ever understand.

For most missionaries, the immediate need, on arriving back home, is to be given time and quiet to adjust not only to jet-lag but also to the speedy transition from one situation into something totally different.

Once relatives have been seen, many missionaries appreciate a week or so away on their own, with time to breathe and to catch up. It is impossible for most of us to begin to understand how hectic their lives will have been prior to returning home. Not only have they had to pack up their belongings, but in some countries they are given the realistic instructions to 'pack as if the country is going to be invaded by an enemy and nothing must be left that could incriminate anyone'. This entails carefully going through papers and burning all that will not be brought home. Then clothes have to be washed scrupulously clean so that insects will find nothing to eat. Everything has to be packed in rat-proof containers, and steps against termites must be taken if things are to be stored where there is any risk of white ants.

The effort of packing up home is exhausting. When you add on handing work over to someone else, or leaving it so that it can be left unattended for furlough months, then you begin to see a weary individual. Pile on to that farewells at the local church, saying goodbye to nationals who have become close friends (whom you may know you may never see again – in some countries they could be dead before you return), plus all the red tape of extricating yourself from some countries, and you may well receive one very exhausted missionary family into your church when they return.

Something like this sounds wonderful: 'Sheila from Bongoland arrives at Gatwick at 5.00 am on Sunday. We could meet her at the airport, take her to her mother's in Birmingham for lunch, and then welcome her at the evening service and let her speak at an after-meeting. Marvellous! She'll know how much we care if we make sure we have her at church the minute she gets to England!'

Yes, your missionary needs to feel very special, and very welcome when he or she arrives back. But it is the rare individual who can cope with a church meeting straight after a long plane flight and all the trauma of leaving one country for another.

Obviously, your missionary must be met at the airport. Sometimes this is done by friends or relatives – but sadly, from time to time people slip through the net. Those who are vulnerable are hurt if no one seems to care enough to meet them after such a long time away. Obviously, the only way to find out if your missionary is going to be met or not is to write and ask, and offer at the same time. There is something very warming and welcoming when you are

packing up your only home into trunks to know that someone cares enough to have planned far ahead to meet you at the airport!

If you can arrange for your missionary to have time away on arrival, it often helps a great deal. Few missionaries have their own homes or the financial resources to go away. This is where you can help – two weeks away, all expenses paid, in cottage, flat, guest house or hotel can make a wonderful and necessary start to a furlough.

If your missionary vaguely says he is going to relatives then do check out tactfully whether he would prefer time on his own before or after this. After a long time away it can be a strain to be with close relatives for too much of the time, too soon. Provide your missionary with the opportunity of time and space to adjust to his home country if he would like it, and you will be doing something very important for his whole family.

The average returning missionary will have been warned by others along these lines: 'Assume that no one is interested in where you've been or what you've been doing. If they ask you then answer in three minutes flat and then ask them about themselves – unless they really want to know, as most people are just being polite.'

Our job is therefore not to pretend that we want to know what they've been doing, but really for us to care very deeply – for only then will we be communicating the truth. If we don't care then we must not pretend we do – but if we have been supporting our missionary in the way to which God has called us to support him, then we will care and want to know as much as he is able to share with us.

Make sure that your missionary has an early chance to debrief. If you as a church have sent him overseas and commissioned him, then he may well expect to report back to you and to share what the Holy Spirit has done through him. If he doesn't expect this, then without making him feel you are checking out whether he has served faithfully or not, make sure that he is able to share his work with you. This sense that others really care is important to a missionary who has suddenly been uprooted and hasn't found his feet at home yet. He will have left behind situations and people that burden him. It is important that you share that load by understanding and by faithfully praying with him for these things – both alone and as a church.

You sent him to a certain situation. While he was there you felt a God-given responsibility (to some extent) for the people to whom he had gone. Just because your missionary has returned on furlough, your responsibility has not decreased – rather it has increased, since he is no longer there and those people may be on their own without any support now.

'Bearing one another's burdens' may be something crucial we can do for certain returning missionaries. If we see a missionary is tired, tense and concerned, and our hearts go out in love, then we can respond with, 'Let me carry your load of concern for those you have left for a little while. Share what you can with me, and I promise to pray daily and as deeply as I'm able to for them. Let me take your burden off you. I'll intercede, you rest, and when you're feeling recovered again, if you want I'll ease off a bit . . .'

Many missionaries are conscientious, caring people who cannot lightly leave behind that for which they have struggled and battled for the past years. Your carrying the load so definitely may give them the spiritual and mental freedom they need for a few weeks. Try it! It could be important!

Learning to change gears in thinking, living and feeling does not happen immediately to the returning missionary. You have sent your missionary overseas as part of your fellowship – now try, as mutual members of the body of

Christ, to understand what this other part is feeling on returning to you again.

New Garments and Old

Having had new clothes made for furlough in the local market, Anne had basked in their glory for a few hours only. Those clothes that had seemed so splendid and up-to-date looked unfinished and amateurish as soon as she was on the plane and compared herself and her family with the others around her. Suddenly she felt she did not fit any more. And it grew worse. As the plane touched down and she arrived at her parents' house she realised that their warm clothes from the tropics that had seemed so thick there, were really too thin and unsuitable.

Again she felt she didn't fit. She was almost a stranger in her parents' home. She knew that she looked different, and that that difference was not particularly glorifying to God. Had she thought it might in some way have brought glory to her Master for her to have hair in a style slightly unusual for Britain, for her children not to wear the kind of shoes English children wore, and for her husband to have an oriental quilted jacket instead of an anorak then she wouldn't have minded the difference. As it was, they were different because they couldn't help it. They had not exercised choice in the matter. They had equipped themselves as best they could, with a very limited budget.

You could express your thanks to your missionary for serving on your behalf overseas by equipping him with furlough clothes. He has gone – sent by you and in your place – to share the Gospel in that land. You could equip him for his time in Britain in the same way that you clothe yourself!

I'll never forget the friend on my last furlough who gave in a way that didn't make me feel like an object of charity.

She was married to a Scripture Union worker and so I knew had slender resources. She made me feel it was fun to go shopping with her and to choose an unusual coat and the sort of luxury nightie that missionary wives wouldn't think of buying – and she somehow made me forget that it was her purse that was emptied by the purchases. Eight years later, I still own that coat and nightie – they are valuable – but far more precious was her way of giving.

A friend once said to me, 'Missionaries all look so dreadful that I think someone ought to take them straight from the airport to the chainstores and get them equipped in modern clothes!'

He had a point! Your missionary would probably jump at the chance of going round the stores with some money, and the freedom to chose new clothes. If he has been living in a tribal situation, or at a time when funds have been very restricted, then part of your blessing him in the Lord for what he has done overseas can be by making the means available for him to enjoy the choice of colours, textures, shapes and styles that our Creative Maker has designed us to appreciate. He may well feel ground down with taking to extremes the right attitude: 'I must be very responsible with the Lord's money entrusted to my use overseas, and mustn't waste anything.' Furlough may be an important time for him to luxuriate in the generosity his Heavenly Father lavishes on him through you.

Adaptation to material standards is hard in changing from one cultural situation to another. Your British missionary may be perplexed, confused and even deeply hurt by things he sees in Britain that he had never noticed before. It may begin on the flight home when he notices the air-hostess getting rid of more food down the waste chute than he has had for his family to eat for a month. That may grieve him. If he has come from a situation where the people he has grown to love dearly have insufficient food then he may not only be hurt but he may be morally indignant and angry at waste in his own culture. Listen to your missionary if he sounds like an Old Testament prophet as he weeps, or thunders out his reactions about the inequality between the people he has left and the country to which he has returned. It is easy to dismiss his deep feelings with a shrug and the attitude, 'He'll get over it, he'll get used to it . . .' If you do this then you may miss something that God is trying to communicate to you through the experience of knowing someone of your own race who has identified with another. He has much with which to enrich you and enlarge your vision.

If together, you and he can sense God's heartbeat and God's concern for those in need in every part of the world then you will be growing together in Christian maturity.

Be tactful and generous when it comes to money. If you take your missionary out to a meal in a restaurant then remember that the tip you leave may be more than a farmer earns in a month in the village where he comes from. Be sensitive to your missionary's feelings!

I believe it is a privilege for a church to be allowed to send one of its members overseas as a missionary. We who give are the richer for giving the one we love to go overseas. God has allowed us to share and actually participate through this one person in his work.

If it is such a privilege then we must guard against any of our missionaries feeling second-rate — that their clothes have to be second-hand, from the sales, or another's cast-offs. Our nation's ambassadors are equipped as befits our Queen — dare we be miserly with those we send in our name to serve the King of Kings?

A Different Culture

In the same way that some people find it hard to adapt to living in a Western materialistic culture after life in the Third World, they also may find it difficult to readjust to other standards we take for granted.

In other cultures a sense of unhurriedness may be important. This is hard to understand, but be patient if your missionary has been immersed in a society where people take the attitude, 'Well, if the train doesn't come today, there'll always be another some time this week!' Such an attitude may actually be regarded as valuable, and punctuality does not matter in some cultures. Be tolerant if your missionary has done so well in identifying with other people that he has shed some of his Western attitudes that are cultural rather than Christian. He will soon remember that it is discourteous to be late!

Living in a culture with different value systems may make him impatient with some Western ideals. Listen to him – he may have something valuable to teach you from another way of coping with life.

Time to Care

Another immediate need our missionary may have on reaching home is for pastoral care and help. If he has been lonely he may need to talk for hours and hours. You can offer something precious to him simply by giving him your ears for as long as he needs to share himself.

If he seems upset about the situation in which he has been living, then listen without too much comment at first. Sometimes people who have been lonely in a foreign country get things blown up out of proportion. You may want to rush to the phone to blow up the director of his missionary society for 'not caring about him better' – but wait! After a few weeks your missionary may see that he himself has been fifty per cent of the trouble that he has faced, and that he needs to get himself sorted out so that he can cope better in future.

On the other hand, there may be times when he shares things with you that no one else knows about. If you feel that as a responsible Christian you must pass this on, then share it prayerfully with your church leader and with him take it to those in authority in the missionary society. Make sure that the whole situation is bathed in prayer, and that you sense God's guidance in bringing certain things into the open. Directors of missionary societies are human – an aggressive approach from you will usually be met by a defensive one from them! On the other hand a gentle and loving attitude of, 'Is there any way we can all work together to get this sorted out as God wants us to?' will usually be met positively.

Some missionaries return home on a spiritual 'high' and others feel as dry as Ezekiel's bones. Churches usually expect to be fed spiritually and to be encouraged by their missionary – and it is right and natural for them to feel like this. However, make sure that your missionary has the time and space for the kind of spiritual renewal and fresh encounter with God that he needs. He may be wounded and tired from the battle, he may be discouraged, he may want to give up, the sacrifice he faces on return may seem more than he can render, or he may quite simply be exhausted in every fibre of his being. Give him the opportunity for renewal.

The money for a Bible correspondence course or a course at Bible college could help meet this need, as also could time away at a Christian retreat centre, or Christian holiday centre. Some missionaries have found the Holy Spirit meeting their needs at conferences like Keswick, Spring Harvest, Filey, the Dales and Downs, Royal Week and so on. Sponsorship for this is often the only way a missionary can afford to go.

If the charismatic renewal has come to your church during the years your missionary has been overseas, then be extra loving about this. Be totally biblical, and correct in your own thinking, and believe the Bible when it says that the Holy Spirit gives his gifts 'as he wills'. Do not allow your missionary to feel substandard if he cannot 'sing in the Spirit' and interpret prophecies the minute he gets off his plane when it is new and strange to him – accustomed as he has been to your solemn services in which he grew up! Do not chase after him trying to make sure he is 'baptised in the Spirit' (or whatever you call what may have happened in your fellowship). If you feel that God longs to break through to him more deeply, then pray earnestly and leave it to God to do as he sees fit! In some situations charismatic issues have proved divisive overseas. Your missionary may have been fighting to hold people of strongly differing views together. In a real sense he may have been one of God's peacemakers – so don't make his heart sink at the prospect of landing in another similarly tricky situation the minute he hits home!

If God has blessed your church with revival while your missionary has been away then pray him into this blessing, rather than force him to decide for or against instantaneously, almost at gun-point.

Be aware that while the 'charismatic divide' is being bridged in Britain this is not so in every other part of the world. If your missionary has been working with missionaries of other nationalities then he may have faced major problems over this that you do not realise are going on! If he is therefore 'prickly' about the subject, be slower to judge him than you would others.

Some missionaries have found their lives have been transformed by being given time by someone who pastors them during furlough. Obviously this needs to be someone as mature, or more mature, than they are – and someone who can be relied on to be totally confidential. A day spent with such a person talking and praying through spiritual needs and issues, and together seeking the Lord has been important to many. Whatever kind of ministry you are used to exercising will usually be appreciated. Although the missionary is usually the one to be giving out, it is important for him to have someone who has the spiritual gift of being able to give to him. The more senior a missionary is, and the more he pastors other missionaries overseas, the more he himself needs pastoring on furlough.

Never feel that your missionary is so spiritual and so perfect that he doesn't need the ordinary kind of pastoring that other sheep in God's flock need. If you think that way, you delude yourself! Your missionary has spiritual needs, deficiences and strengths in the same way that each member of the body of Christ has them!

Keeping in Touch

Having taken care of your missionary's immediate needs (a bit like helping someone when they come out of hospital) you can then work at long-term needs.

Ideally your missionary should not hit the UK unprepared. You should keep him in touch with his home culture, so that when he comes back it is less of a shock than it would otherwise be. Provided he is able both to indentify with the new culture to which he has been sent, and also to maintain his cultural identity as 'British' (as nationals of his new country will always see him) he will be grateful for links with his homeland.

You can keep him in touch and at the same time give him opportunities to relax and have a bit of fun while he is overseas. A weekly newspaper sent out by air, plus secular magazines, will be widely read by many. Also appreciated will be your denominational newspaper, and a selection of Christian magazines. Make sure that he does get a *selection* – his view of the church will be lop-sided should he receive only *Restoration* or *Buzz*! He needs to understand what is happening in the nation and in the Church as a whole. He will return to find a jungle through which he cannot hack a path to understanding unless you help clear the way for him.

Knowing what is happening in British society is vital for him on return. Trends in society are reported regularly in CARE News, the magazine of CARE Trust, and this might help him – especially if he has children to be affected by society. Cassettes from the London Institute for Contemporary Christianity or from the British L'Abri Fellowship will also help him understand trends towards secularism and pluralism and how this is affecting the thinking of ordinary British Christians. It is good to make sure he knows about current favourite TV programmes – but it is even more important to ensure that he understands what the thinking behind television programming is doing to the way society behaves. (If you don't know this yourself, you'll find it doubly worthwhile learning, to pass on to him!)

Your missionary should not be left unaware of major parliamentary debates that affect Christian thinking – discussion of the Abortion law, the Matrimonial Proceedings Bill, the Obscenity law, unemployment, racism, education etc. If you are feeding him regularly with both Christian and secular material then he will know about the contemporary music scene, the media and other factors influencing the thinking of the nation to which he has returned. Similarly he will know of the crazes and fads, the fashions and foibles of his home country.

Having looked on from outside through reading, he will

enter a country that he knows about intellectually, and the strangeness will be more emotional than mental.

A Place to Call Home

An obvious need when a missionary returns from overseas is that of accommodation. This needs careful, prayerful and creative thought. A few missionaries already have their own homes, or have inherited the money with which to buy a home but they are in the minority. You may discover that your missionary has been living overseas in mission property or in rented accommodation all his missionary career. Probably he accepts this without resentment. He accepts that he follows a Master who had 'nowhere to lay his head'. He is quietly glad to be like Jesus and not to be encumbered with property overseas.

This means that he has nowhere in the whole world that he can regard as 'home' – he *belongs* nowhere. God has implanted within most women the 'nesting instinct'. It is right and natural for women – married and single – to have a deep-seated need for a home in which they belong. There is nothing that sets missionary women apart from the rest of humanity and makes them devoid of this deep instinct. There is nothing, moreover, that makes an unmarried missionary woman less feminine than her married counterpart – she needs a home as much as the married does. Missionary children will feel the need for a secure base very deeply.

Your church could do something special for your missionary by making a real home available. Is it really out of the question that you as a fellowship should buy a home for your missionary? You buy a home for yourself. Is it beyond the realms of possibility that you should consider supplying your missionary with the security and deep joy of knowing that he does have somewhere where he belongs – a place to which he can go on furloughs, a place to which his children can go when they are at university in Britain and separated from him, a place to which he can return should he suddenly have to leave his work overseas, and a place to which he can retire? Your missionary may not consciously want such a place – but it is possible that it would be something very special for him should you supply it – and maintain it and rent it out while he is overseas. It is asking a lot – but when you send him abroad you call on him to sacrifice a great deal on your behalf!

'Home' doesn't need to be vast – even a caravan, or a one-roomed flat can be of inestimable value to the single girl overseas. It gives her a valid alternative to spending furlough with relatives should she want an option, or moving from place to place, putting down no roots anywhere in the world, and having no place of retreat that she can creatively turn into her very own home.

Families who have opened up their homes to missionaries

on furlough have also done something very wonderful. Those who have integrated other families into their own are much appreciated. But do find out what kind of person your missionary is. He may want to be with others, or he may need to be on his own during furlough. Usually a missionary family (after running an open house overseas) needs privacy to consolidate their family togetherness and to build the strength they need for the tasks ahead. Missionary marriages may have been put under considerable stress by the situation overseas and the lack of privacy, and couples may need time alone to communicate again, to talk through past hurts and misunderstandings and to strengthen their joint spiritual life.

Ideally, if your church cannot provide a home for each of its missionaries (and I suggest that very seriously as an ideal) then it ought to think seriously of providing some kind of furlough accommodation. Some churches own houses or flats which are made available to their missionaries. You can safely assume that your missionary will be profoundly grateful if you make this accommodation available rent and rate free. If you study your missionary's allowance on furlough, in most cases you will be appalled at the small amount he has to live on. This is not due to missionary societies being stingy – it is because income rarely keeps up with inflation, and overseas workers cannot be left without the money for food and essentials!

Do not always expect your missionary to be very good at maintaining this furlough accommodation. In most cases, housing overseas is so different from that in Britain that he simply has not gained the DIY skills needed for the UK scene. Also remember that he probably has a heavy speaking programme or study course to cram into his time on leave, and that he has returned for rest and recreation! If you can take house maintenance right out of his hands he will be most grateful. It is even better if there is someone in the church he can phone when a drain-pipe is blocked, the central heating will not go on, or the washing machine breaks down. Do try to save him heavy repair bills. Possibly your church could employ someone who is unemployed to be 'on call' for a missionary household for odd jobs.

Most churches that provide accommodation for their missionaries will give it a good clean for their return. It is so appreciated by a tired mother if she can walk into a clean home with everything in working order, and collapse without having to set to with scrubbing brush as soon as she gets off the plane.

A special bonus could be a love-gift of a full deep freeze, and a pantry full of basics and plenty of tinned goods. A bathroom cupboard stocked with essentials from toothpaste down to sticking plaster would be a lovely surprise! And one or two very special luxuries to delight a woman's heart could make someone feel really cherished and cared for, both by you and by her loving Heavenly Father who is showering his love on her through you. How about thinking of the kinds of things she can neither find nor afford in many missionary situations – a gift set of soap, talc, bathsalts and perfume; a beautiful nightie; handcream? Such creative love will make her feel special to you but more than that it will surround her with a sense of God's unique value placed on her.

Make sure that your missionary returns to a warm flat or house, with beds made up and nothing needing doing for a few days. Several meals already prepared (in the deep freeze if there is one), and one ready to eat on arrival will be more than appreciated.

Remember that those coming from the tropics will need extra heating and bedding, and supply this. If you can help with the heating bills it will mean that they dare turn on the heating, where otherwise in the interests of economy they may be reluctant to do so, fearing they will run out of funds too quickly.

If you have a single missionary living with you then make sure that he or she has adequate privacy. Don't allow your children access to his or her bedroom. Try to make your missionary feel that he is neither a guest nor a lodger – make sure he knows that your home is his home, and he is welcome to entertain his friends in it. Make sure that he is able to have people in for meals without necessarily eating with your family when they are there. Let him live an independent life while he is with you – but make sure he does not feel cut off from you!

If someone is living with you, then include him in all your family activities but do not force him into something he does not really want to do. Help him to feel both that he belongs to you but also that he is free from obligation to you and can be as independent as he wishes. A fine balance – but one achieved by many host families!

A Car is Vital

Transport is always a major headache for those returning missionaries who have not had help with it. To enable your missionary to achieve all he needs to in the short time he is home, and to be adequately rested for return, he is going to need a car. This is one of those things he will not be able to afford to buy. Some churches have a 'missionary car' they are able to make available free of charge to furlough missionaries. Others buy a car for their missionaries, and sometimes generous church members who are a two-car family lend one for the duration of furlough.

Do not buy your missionary a bargain secondhand car that is going to cost him so much in repairs when it breaks down that he runs out of money. Do not lumber him with the worry of an old car that is unreliable. If you can buy him a brand new car – as some churches have sacrificially done – then that is ideal! Give him something you would gladly run yourself – and not your own cast-off that you are discarding because it is giving you problems. (If this sounds obvious then I am sorry – but all these things have happened to friends of mine and their furlough cars!)

If you are able to handle road tax, insurance, and garage bills so that your missionary does not have to cope with this then you will be giving him an added bonus – and also you will be releasing money from the slender resources of missionary societies for overseas work. Remember that most societies try to keep home expenses to the bare minimum to channel as much money overseas as is possible.

If the missionary husband is travelling on speaking engagements and needs the car, do make sure that wife and children have transport, and are not marooned at home.

The subject of missionaries and their children generates much heat and little light – especially from those least qualified to speak with authority on the subject!

If you are providing accommodation for a missionary family then you may want to think through some assumptions that are found in some church circles. There are those who believe that missionary children as a race are undisciplined savages, who will rip a home to shreds and therefore should be given the most battered and least destructible things to use in the home provided for them. Careful study of missionary children will prove this to be unfounded – the exceptions to this rule are, of course, the ones everyone talks about and remembers!

It is important that missionary children – especially those used to living very simply in a Third World situation – should know how to behave and how to treat things on the British scene. If they do not learn on furlough then they may well have no opportunity to learn that beautiful things need treating carefully, and that God their Creator has put them in a world full of beauty which they are not to pollute and destroy. In many Third World situations it is not possible for this lesson to be learned properly – furlough may be a good chance.

Therefore, contrary to common sense, you may want to make sure that the home to which your missionary family goes is not filled with furniture that no one wants, carpets dug out of someone's attic, and old rubbish that can get broken without anyone minding. The attitude with which you make a lovely home available to a missionary family, however, needs to be such that the mother will not feel guilty when her children scratch the furniture, spill dark brown drinks on the carpet and drop a beautiful vase. An attitude of 'this is the Lord's, for you to use. If anything gets broken or spoiled he understands – and you're not answerable to us' may help.

But be sensitive! If your missionary family is one of those where the parents *really* feel they could not cope with their tribe in anything that cannot be ruined, then give them a home that *can* be destroyed! However, such a family is rarely seen nowadays.

'This is the Lord's house and we want to equip it for his servants as if we are equipping it for him' is the lovely attitude of some churches towards furlough accommodation. Missionary wives and singles will much appreciate matching co-ordinated colour schemes, beautiful furniture, real china and some of the things we take for granted that they lack overseas. 'Why should we give the Lord's ambassadors anything second-rate?' is the attitude of some churches to equipping a home with everything from steam iron, to TV, to toys for the children. But do not get so carried away that the home you provide is uncomfortably luxurious and too expensive for someone on a missionary income to run!

Some missionary children will be confused by all that has happened to them in a short space of time. They may miss national friends, servants, and the way of life to which they have been accustomed. Be patient if a fractious child arrives – and take him or her off mother's hands for a few hours if appropriate.

Schooling has to be arranged for missionary children on furlough, and this usually needs to be done before the children arrive in the UK to ensure that there is a place for them. Write beforehand to let your missionaries know about school facilities and options, find out their preferences, and offer to make arrangements if they would like you to. Obviously one person in the church needs to take this in hand rather than several, to avoid confusion.

Baby-sitters can be a bonus, so that missionary husbands

and wives can attend church events and social functions together, or just have an evening out together – something they are unlikely to be able to do in their missionary situation. The gift of meal–vouchers for a local restaurant could transform a penniless anniversary into a unique occasion for a missionary couple.

Do be careful to avoid getting over-involved in the debate as to whether or not your missionaries should return overseas when their children reach the age of requiring schooling in the UK. Many thousands of conflicting words are offered to missionary parents at this stage in their careers, and the most well–meaning advice tends to be ill-timed and even hurtful. Be ready to give your opinion if it is asked, but make sure your missionary parents know that it is only your opinion, that you could be wrong in what you are saying, and that whatever they decide you will back them fully.

Of far more help than your words are your prayers. Ask God to burden you for those children, to so impress you with their needs that you will intercede for them. Then continually ask the Holy Spirit to make his way clear to the parents. Trust him to do just that without your manipulation.

If you really feel a God-given resonsibility to say something to your missionary parents about their responsibility to their children, then it is usually best to do this through your church leaders. If the church leadership agrees with you, then it is a matter to be taken up at this level, since a deeply-held feeling that a church cannot support the return of a missionary family overseas is a major matter that needs examining and discussing carefully in consultation with your missionary's missionary society.

Real Friends

Your missionary may not only feel like a fish out of water because of culture shock, but he may also feel acutely the lack of any real friends. Do make sure that he is surrounded by the warmth and love of people who really do care about him – and people about whom he can feel the same.

Single missionaries will have differing needs at different stages of their lives. Each needs to feel that he or she belongs and really matters to someone. He needs to know that he is accepted as he is, and is of value and importance to just one person. Obviously, for the single person this is not going to be through a marriage partner and you must sensitively assess whether your missionary's need for some close relationship is being met.

Understand that many single missionary women go through an acutely painful stage mid-career when they realise that they probably are never going to get married. They may have soldiered on for years never really thinking that they will not get married, and always assuming that in his time God will give them a partner. Then the crunch time comes when they can see that this is not to be. Other singles may pass through repeated crises at different stages in their careers – when their longing for marriage seems overwhelming. This is normal and natural, and your understanding love at such times will help a great deal.

The single missionary who returns for furlough after the death of a remaining parent will feel the pain of bereavement deeply. He or she may feel at a deep level. 'I don't really matter to anyone any more – there's no one left . .' You can help heal that pain of loss by your creative loving.

Some missionaries feel that during their time overseas their brains have stagnated and intellectually they have stuck in the same rut. They may long to grow during furlough and to develop in different ways. Courses are available that will help with this – ranging from local education authority courses, to Open University courses, to Bible correspondence courses and a variety of professional courses. These can be residential, by correspondence, or at night school. Some are specifically for missionaries on furlough; certain Bible colleges and theological colleges run refresher courses, and specific furlough training is also available for missionary doctors and nurses.

If you sense that your missionary is in a rut then gently encourage him to take up a further course of study – and make sure that he has a grant from the local education authority, or from your church, to cover the cost of it.

It may be that your missionary most needs the refreshment of creativity – learning a new skill like journalism, pottery, typing, dressmaking or cooking could be more important to a tired mind than cramming it with facts relating to his overseas work. Maybe he needs the opportunity for sport – riding, sailing, water-skiing, pony trekking, mountaineering or learning to parachute jump. If you can finance him to do something like this then you could be contributing to his overall rehabilitation for returning to the hard slog of his overseas work.

And, in many ways, that is what furlough is all about – getting your missionary totally refreshed and recreated ready for the next long haul overseas. Probably you see his furlough from a different angle – your own – of how to use him to the maximum advantage to inspire and encourage others to support overseas mission. That too is important, but the church in the UK has tended to over-emphasise this aspect for too long and half-killed its furlough missionaries in the process. That is not what furlough is supposed to achieve!

Making the Best Use of Your Missionary's Furlough

Sensible planning on your part, working closely with the missionary society, can make the most of your missionary's furlough. Remember that in many cases the missionary society exercises tight control over its furlough missionaries and works out itineraries with and for them, leaving them little time for their own home churches. If you feel that you need your missionary to be part of you, and perhaps even to work on the church pastoral team for a few months, then put this idea to your missionary about a year and a half before furlough is due. This may seem too far ahead for anyone to make such plans but in reality missionaries who are gifted speakers will be booked for important meetings over a year before their furloughs – and it may be too late for them to spend the time in their local church that they and you would really like, unless you plan well in advance.

Having your missionary serve as part of the pastoral team for a couple of months can be invaluable both to the missionary (in being integrated back into the church) and in helping church members to get to know him in such a way that it is easy and natural for them to continue support when he returns overseas. Many missionary societies will gladly co-operate with churches in making such schemes possible, and free their missionaries from speaking tours for that time.

Most missionaries have to spend time travelling around the country, sharing news of their work and raising support. Back them up in this. If you feel that their schedule is too heavy and they are responsible themselves for setting up more than they can really manage, then tactfully tell them so. If their missionary society is asking too much of them, remember it will not help them to accept this situation (which they cannot change) without resentment, if you keep on making them feel they are being over-worked and abused. Find a way of tactfully communicating your feelings to the missionary society, so that your missionary will not get a black mark for grumbling, but the point will be taken and hopefully other missionaries will be saved from a similar situation in the future.

Some furlough missionaries thrive on mammoth speaking tours and are able to exercise a public speaking ministry in a way that they cannot overseas. If this is so, make sure your missionary has your moral backing – and above all is supported by your prayers for every meeting he takes. Let him report back to you after tours, and make sure he knows that you are interested in what God is doing through him on furlough. If he has a student ministry on furlough then give him the extra support he will need on returning, after the heavy demands the students will have made on him. Never let him feel alone on a furlough ministry – or that you regard him as superhuman and somehow able to cope with a schedule designed to kill the toughest!

Not all missionaries are gifted speakers, and some feel failures on furlough. They see their colleagues in great demand all over the country and feel hopeless and worthless when they panic at the thought of having to speak to the handful of elderly ladies at an afternoon women's meeting, or the local prayer meeting of a dozen ardent supporters. If you are doing your job right, your missionary should feel of such value to you that it will not really enter his head that you might judge him on furlough performance and find him wanting – and in his own eyes a failure. He ought to know by all you have been to him that he is loved and valued for himself – and that you accept him for what he is rather than for what he does.

The shyest missionary, handled lovingly and gently, will have an important contribution to make in your church home groups, chatting over coffee, without ever needing to be stuck up in the pulpit.

Missionaries who love speaking in public may well be delighted to be more widely available. Some have contributed to religious education or current affairs courses in local schools – but they need warning that while they can share personal experiences they must not try to convert or proselytise or the school will be in trouble.

Others have a contribution to make on local radio, on television, in the local newspaper or in the national religious or secular press. Rotary clubs, business men's lunches, the Christian Women's luncheon clubs, school speech days, and many women's secular organisations may all have an opening for your missionary provided you come up with an angle that your missionary could cover that is of general interest and does not sound too religious. Christianity will come in as a natural part of the talk or in the question and answer time afterwards. Someone is bound to ask, 'What made you give everything up to go and do that?' This kind of speaking may refresh your missionary and may give him a sense of self-esteem that is important for him to gain during furlough – but don't let him kill himself off in the excitement and thrill of being used by God for evangelism in his home land. Make sure he is fit to return.

If your missionary has an interesting story, the media

could be very interested in him. If he is ready for this kind of exposure then you could contact a Christian in the local press or national media to find out how best to handle it. A note of caution: for important reasons his missionary society may not want him to go public on certain matters, either for internal missionary society reasons or because it could cause political problems overseas for not only that missionary but for the national Christian church in the land from which he has come. Do not enthusiastically rush in until you have carefully checked this out. Your missionary may be unaware of sensitive areas and be more naive about this than you realise. Double check to be really sure, with his missionary society. Were missionaries to be expelled from 'his' country, or national Christians to be put into jail because of something he said you would more than regret it – and it is too late to be wise after such an event.

Hopefully, by the end of his furlough you all will have identified very closely with your missionary and his family, so that you are more one in the body of Christ than you were before. Hopefully you will send him back secure in the knowledge that God is loving him through you, and that you care for him and will support him the more strongly for the time he has been with you. Hopefully, his concerns will be the more yours, so that he knows you will support financially, prayerfully, emotionally and practically. Hopefully, he will know that should a crisis occur he can trust you to care for any dependent relatives he has left behind. Hopefully, he will know beyond any doubt that not only has God commissioned him to go, but also that you have sent him, and that you and he are one in Christ in the venture and adventure to which God has jointly called you all.

Missionary Outreach Today

Stanley Davies

What is really happening in missions today? Are missionaries still needed when the church in some countries is growing at such a phenomenal rate? Are missions a relic of a past era which should be phased out now that there are national churches in most countries of the world? These and many other questions are being asked by thinking Christians. They need clear answers.

What is Happening Around the World

Phenomenal Growth

Around the world there are certain countries where the Church has grown at an extraordinary rate. In Latin America the evangelical churches are becoming a major force in the countries of Brazil, Guatemala, Chile and El Salvador. The largest Protestant sanctuary in the world has been built in Brazil by the Brazil For Christ denomination: its seating capacity is 25,000. Various Brazilian groups are reported to have planted nearly three thousand new evangelical congregations in recent years.

In sub-Saharan Africa the development of vibrant churches from Ethiopia to Liberia, from Uganda to South Africa has been dramatic. That growth has produced its own set of problems and challenges but it is a significant fact that has taken place during this century.

Certain parts of Asia have witnessed the development of churches that now represent considerable proportions of the populations of their countries. In Korea there are more studying theology in Protestant seminaries than in all of Europe and Africa combined. In Indonesia there are about twenty-five million Christians in a predominantly Muslim country. In Singapore it is estimated that about thirty per cent of all university students claim to be Christian.

In China the communist government official figures for the number of Protestant Christians in that country is three million. This alone would be phenomenal growth, as this is over four times the number of Protestant Christians who were recorded at the time of the withdrawal of missionary personnel in the early 1950s. (Similar increases are also reported as having taken place amongst those from Catholic churches.) Careful analysis of reports from China show that the number may even exceed twenty million. This is in the face of what has been described as the most intensive attack on the Church in any century.

In the light of these encouraging signs, some Christians in the West feel that the day of Western missions is over. It may be wise for some agencies to re-deploy their forces, but the sharing of resources and personnel will continue for as long as mutual assistance is seen to be needed and valued. This assistance must in no way become a restrictive burden or a strait-jacket upon the recipients of such assistance.

However in many countries where dramatic growth has taken place, the needs of the young Church are for help in Bible teaching and training programmes, the development of literature programmes, and the provision of training specialists in many different fields. Church leaders are requesting assistance from churches with greater experience in such matters. Dare we turn a deaf ear to the plea for help from young churches that are seeing phenomenal growth that needs particular assistance where we can provide it?

The Growth of Emerging Missions

Along with the growth of the Church in many parts of the world, there is a growing understanding that each church has the responsibility to fulfill the commands of Christ to make disciples of all nations. This has not always been the case. Tragically some churches founded by Western missions failed to appreciate the dynamic nature of the Christian faith and of their own responsibility to be witnesses to their own Jerusalem, Judea, Samaria and the ends of the earth, as outlined by the Lord himself in Acts 1:8. Sometimes that failure was due to a blind spot in missionary strategy that gave the impression that mission was the prerogative of the

Western churches with their greater resources and Christian heritage.

Today, however, there is an increasing army of missionaries from every part of the globe that is swelling the numbers of missionaries who are crossing cultural and linguistic boundaries to take the Gospel to those who have never heard it. In 1960 only three per cent of all Protestant missionaries were non-Western. In 1984 that percentage is almost twenty per cent. If the present trend continues, by the end of the century the percentage could be as much as forty per cent of the total Protestant missionary force around the world. This is a tremendous step forward as the truly international nature of the Church is reflected in teams of missionaries from different parts of the world.

The strategic value of this factor should be obvious to all. Where such international teams exist, no longer can the accusation be made that missionaries are Western imperialists, nor that the Christian Gospel is simply a Western religion. When different team members from such diverse countries as Korea, Japan, Brazil, India, or Nigeria are present alongside members from Europe or America, the claim of the Gospel – that it is for all people and truly breaks down the barriers erected by human suspicion and prejudice – can be seen to be real. This internationalising of missionary teams is not an easy matter. It is costly in terms of learning from one another, preferring one another in love, when all and each appreciate their own cultural heritage, but it is a living demonstration of the power of the Gospel.

Lawrence Keyes in his book *The Last Age of Mission* has documented some of the recent developments in emerging missions from different parts of the world, which had been looked on traditionally by Western Christians as mission fields in themselves. New missionary societies are coming into being with names that are new to Christians in the

West. The Evangelical Missionary Society, which is the missionary arm of 'The Evangelical Churches of West Africa', now has over 580 missionaries serving with that particular group; the Friends Missionary Prayer Band based in Madras, South India, has over 170 missionaries; the Indonesian Missionary Fellowship has over 200 missionaries. These will give an idea of the growing missionary force that God is raising up around the world.

Multi-Mission Teams

Together with the development of emerging missions, another trend in recent years is the coming together of several mission and Church agencies to work under a united team. Such an approach has been made in Nepal, where many different mission agencies co-operate in the United Mission to Nepal, which is able to co-ordinate the activities from different parts of the world. This approach has much to commend it, since it ensures that there is a co-ordinated approach to government, while also allowing for strategic planning of ministries. No one agency has the resources, personnel or finance for such an undertaking.

A similar approach was made in the Sudan, when different agencies responded to the needs of that area following the devastation of the civil war. The ACROSS team of workers, with their varied skills drawn from many nations, and funded by several agencies from around the globe, have brought together a team of dedicated Christian workers who have been able to provide a service that has been appreciated by both government and the local people.

On a smaller scale, many mission and Church agencies are finding this method to be most beneficial, particularly where a project is too large for any one group to cope with.

Missionary Prayer Meeting. Standing Room Only

Where Are the Needs?

It is vital to keep things in perspective when looking at those areas of the world where growth has taken place in the churches. For in many other parts of the world the Church is tiny, weak and introspective, and in some countries there are no known Christians and no churches of national believers.

The Remaining Unreached Peoples of the World

Large areas of North Africa and the Middle East, of Central Asia, East Asia and many lands now under Marxist government contain many groups of people who have been largely untouched by the Gospel. These will mainly be people who are followers of the Islamic, Hindu or Buddhist religions.

Grim statistics still challenge the churches around the world. Over two thousand million people have no church in their own culture to reveal Christ.

Many thousands of villages and towns of Southern Europe have little or no witness to the love of Christ. The Bible is a closed book. Various hindrances, such as formalised religion of one kind or another, the acceptance of a militant atheism by a growing number of their youth, or a tragic blindness through rampant materialism, produce apathy or indifference to the Gospel. There is an urgent need to reappraise priorities so that evangelism is made a priority in an area that once had flourishing churches in a former era.

We need to be aware that the world population does not remain static. At present it stands at 4,600 million and on present estimates may reach 6,000 million by the year 2000. In pure percentage terms the proportion of people in the world who are Christians is slipping back even though there are more Christians living on earth today than there have ever been in the history of the world. The challenge of vast population increases in different parts of the world is a solemn reminder of our continuing need to bring the Gospel to each and every generation.

Urbanisation

The cities of our world are growing at an alarming rate. In the last century the vast majority of people lived in a rural situation. By the year 2000 it is predicted on current trends that percentages of people living in cities will be as follows: Western Europe 82 per cent; USSR and Eastern Europe 80 per cent; USA 94 per cent; Latin America 73 per cent; Asia

60 per cent; Africa 45 per cent. This will mean that Mexico City could be as large as 30 million, Calcutta 19 million, Cairo 16 million, Seoul 18 million, Lagos 9 million, to give just a few examples.[1]

The churches must develop new strategies to reach these cities for Christ. It is totally unacceptable for Christians to retreat into the pleasant rural areas, abandoning the cities to secular and godless forces. Urban mission will mean a costly involvement amongst the grim deprivation often found in inner city areas. The complexity of the task is enormous, as the majority of cities have attracted many diverse groups of people. Raymond Bakke, Lausanne coordinator for Urban Ministry, is one who has made a study of reaching people in urban centres. In a study of European capital cities he demonstrated how those cities which once served as administrative centres for empires in the heyday of the colonial era now house large numbers of formerly colonised people. The dynamics of this process have created enormous problems for old urban establishments in London, Paris, Amsterdam and Berlin, but at the same time they also create exciting new opportunities for urban ministry and cross-cultural evangelism.

The concrete jungles of our world with their inner city ghettos and sprawling shanty towns require new initiatives by Christians committed to show the love of Christ by their actions as well as to speak of the deliverance that only Christ can bring. The development of Christian communities in the towering city blocks where alienation, fear, hatred and isolation are the experience of so many is a task that the best and ablest missionaries need to give attention to. This is perhaps as great a missionary challenge to the resources, perseverance and commitment of the Church as were the continental coastlands in the early nineteenth

[1] See *The Future of World Evangelization*, edited by Edward R. Dayton and Samuel Wilson (MARC, 1984).

century and the continental inland areas in the late nine-teenth century.

Some of these groups of people, now in Europe, come from countries closed to normal missionary activity. They may be geographically reachable, but we must devise suitable strategies to approach such communities. One such way is the re-deployment of missionaries who once served in distant areas of the world but whose missions have been led to reassign them to work amongst those who for different reasons now live in Europe. For example, there are over 1,600,000 Turks in Germany and 250,000 Vietnamese in France, and in the British Isles there are significant communities from India and Pakistan who have their own treasured languages, cultural identity and religion.

International Students

The universities of Great Britain as well as other developed countries of the Western world have attracted many students from other continents. The responsibility of Christians to extend a welcome to such international students is vital. Too many return to their own countries having been given a cold shoulder with no invitation to a Christian home. The work of the UCCF Overseas Students Department and the efforts of those working together with the Churches Commission for Overseas Students provide various ways by which Christians can show genuine friendship and help in the early months of an international student's stay in Britain. Hospitality schemes, cultural evenings and practical assistance programmes provide a poignant reminder of the relevance of the words of Christ, 'I was a stranger and you welcomed me' (Matthew 25:35).

One of the ways that help can be given is by the provision of accommodation. This is particularly acute for those with families and in the major cities of Britain.

Another group that visits Britain is the increasing wave of students who have a desire to master the English language. Efforts by some churches on the south coast of England to introduce them to Christ during their brief stay in this country are an attempt to use this opportunity in a creative way.

Analysing the Task

A clearer identification of the task remaining to be accomplished has been given to us by various groups conducting research and analysing the needs of different parts of our world. The monumental study by David Barratt and his team in Nairobi has produced *The World Christian Encyclopædia*, which gives a clear assessment of Christianity in every country of the world.

The ministry of MARC (Missions Advanced Research Communications Centre) is helping to identify, continent by continent, the different groups of people still without a witness. The activities of the Lausanne Committee for World Evangelisation, giving help in strategic planning to different groups of Christians in many parts of the world, have led to significant advance in bringing together Christians in a given area to work together to achieve the task of evangelisation. At a more popular level, the production of *Operation World* by Patrick Johnstone and his research team at WEC International headquarters has made many of these facts available to Christians in local churches. His ministry is also greatly appreciated by mission leaders in providing most helpful analytical studies of different areas of the world.

All of these are only aids to making the basic facts known to Christians. These facts need to be interpreted and acted upon, so that people without a living church in their midst may soon understand the good news for themselves.

Who are the Workers?

The Present Missionary Force

The present Protestant missionary force in the world
includes about 55,000 from North America, 17,000 from
the two-thirds world and 13,000 from Europe. There are
also significant numbers from Australia, New Zealand
and South Africa. Of the European contingent about
five thousand are from Great Britain. It will be seen,
therefore, that the contribution to the total missionary force
from Great Britain is quite small, but still important.
British missionaries need to realise that when they serve
their Lord overseas they may well be outnumbered particularly by their North American colleagues and will be
working alongside a growing number from the two-thirds
world.

These figures represent those who are sent through a
recognised missionary society or by direct arrangement
from the sending church in one country to a church in
another country. Such workers are sometimes referred to
as fraternal workers. These arrangements are likely to
continue particularly with a growing awareness amongst
the House Church movement of the need to be involved in
world mission. However a note of caution needs to be
sounded at this point. The wealth of experience gained by
missionary societies over many decades has provided a fund
of knowledge that should not be ignored. It is one thing to
send a person overseas, it is quite another matter to ensure
that he has been adequately trained and prepared for a
cross-cultural ministry. The need for adequate orientation,
language study and for pastoral care while on the field of
service as well as in the home country are matters that must
be thought through carefully.

The diversity of types of ministries is staggering because
the task of mission is complex. The variety of opportunities

advertised by societies shows that there is no lack of vacancies. The UCCF publication *Jobs Abroad*, a termly bulletin, lists over three thousand vacancies of interest to Christians.

Missions are still recruiting those with professional qualifications in the educational, medical and technical fields at all levels. However, those with experience in agriculture and community development are in great demand. All teams of missionary personnel require those with administrative and management skills, together with those who can provide back-up service to those in remote areas. Specialists in the communication field of radio, television and allied audio-visual ministries are needed. Not all those listed above need to be linguistic experts, though these are still required. However an effective missionary is one who has a desire to communicate the love of Christ to those among whom he is ministering and to whom he has been sent. That desire will only be turned into reality as a missionary learns to communicate in the language of the people. Language provides one of the keys to understanding culture and needs to be mastered so as to be faithful to the task of accurately communicating the eternal truth of God in a way that is comprehensible and meaningful to the hearer. There are no short cuts to this discipline.

Tentmakers

Many countries do not easily welcome the Christian missionary. Some are hard to enter. However, there are usually more ways into a house than through the front door.

Ever since Pentecost, Christians have shared their faith wherever they have gone. During the era of Roman rule there was considerable freedom to travel for commercial reasons, on military business or as an official of the empire. This freedom allowed for the spread of the Christian message by Christians in all walks of life and every profession. We do well to remember that the Church in Antioch was founded by anonymous Christians who moved there most probably for business reasons, following the persecution of the Church in Jerusalem.

The Moravian Christians used this method. They sent artisans and craftsmen to be self-supporting missionaries to the West Indies, Greenland and many other parts of the world.

Those with professional qualifications in medicine, education, engineering or agriculture are able to apply for the many job opportunities advertised in the national press in such countries as Libya, Iraq, Saudi Arabia, Somalia, China or Mozambique. Opportunities in commerce, with the United Nations Organisation, in the Diplomatic Corps or the armed services give unique openings for Christians to be involved as faithful witnesses to Jesus Christ. Such people need the prayerful support of their home churches, training in the basic skills of cross–cultural communication, and an understanding of the culture and religion of the area where they are working. This vast resource of Christian people is largely overlooked. Far more attention needs to be given by local churches and mission councils to involving those going overseas on business to be thoroughly eqipped for the ministry they could exercise.

Another way of making Christ known is by encouraging those wishing to continue their studies at university to do so in a university overseas. Postgraduate courses are available for those with specialised studies in such diverse places as Istanbul, Cairo, Bucharest or Karachi. The average missionary does not have regular contact with groups of students in such universities and yet these are the future leaders of the countries that need to be reached for Christ.

As one reads mission history a striking feature of some of the earlier pioneers was their youthfulness. For example, Hudson Taylor was only twenty-one years old when he first went to China as a missionary, and thirty-three years old when he founded the China Inland Mission. George Verwer, the International Director of Operation Mobilisation, was in his early twenties when God led him to be involved in calling together young people for mission. Today many young people are again being challenged to participate in God's mission to a lost and needy world. Their drive and enthusiasm needs to be tempered and harnessed alongside older and more experienced workers who can channel their energies in creative and meaningful service and witness. The development world-wide of Operation Mobilisation and Youth with a Mission has been a channel through which many youngsters have been exposed to and involved in Christian ministry in different parts of the world. Their success has often been linked to their wholehearted commitment to sacrificial service and simple life-style. There are millions around the world who today can thank God for the ministry of such dedicated teams of young people through whom they first heard the Good News of Jesus Christ. Today these missions are using their teams to provide on-the-job training. Such training is constantly being reviewed, revised and improved.

It is significant that many missionary societies are now arranging their own programmes to involve young people on a short term/volunteer basis. Many of these young people are radically changed in their understanding of mission after one visit to a country overseas. Some find their way to further training in preparation for longer term involvement in the world, whereas others return to their home churches and often provide the stimulus and enthusiasm needed for local evangelistic outreach.

The ease of travel to remote areas of the world compared to a few decades ago is likely to increase this kind of involvement by young people. Missions must be aware of the potential to involve and expose young people in such programmes. This will require adaptation of long established patterns by missionary societies but will in the end prove to be beneficial both to those involved in the programmes and those who will be able to be reached by such youthful energies.

The short-term programmes that have proliferated in recent years are likely to continue to be a major factor in missions in the next decade. These programmes allow Christians with particular skills to serve the Lord for specific periods of time (between one and four years) and enable them to be involved in ministries alongside those who know the culture and language. In our modern world there will be very few career missionaries who remain in one location for a lifetime as in former generations. The speed of change is increasing. The need for adaptability and flexibility is a priority.

Along with the short termers there is a continuing need for those who will train and equip themselves adequately in patient language acquisition and cultural adaptation, while gaining the respect of the communities to whom they minister. A combination of both short-term and long-term missionary involvement is a factor that all mission agencies must come to terms with, harnessing the energies and expertise of younger workers with those of greater experience.

Which is the Right View of Mission?

The meaning of mission continues to be debated by theologians, missiologists, church growth experts and mission strategists.

Various Definitions

Many attempts have been made to define mission. Some would limit it to evangelism and relegate the work of social concern and relief and development to a very secondary position. At the other end of the spectrum some are advocating the need to develop dialogue with those of different religious views to gain an understanding of the truth that they have received.

Those who would seek to emphasise the need for dialogue rather than mission sometimes do so on the basis that for them the term mission has unfortunate overtones. The great stress is on learning from the Muslim or Hindu and seeking to discover the truth. No one would deny the need for careful listening and honest sharing, though this has sometimes been neglected in the past. There may still be a few well-meaning missionaries who fit the cartoons on 'How to do Mission' by broadcasting the message from a hot-air balloon while having no contact with or tangible understanding of their audience. However, those who advocate dialogue as the best way forward come very close to being willing to barter the content of the message they have received in the pursuit of truth. Christians have been entrusted with a message that is non-negotiable. Certainly the way it is expressed must be appropriate, and seen to be understood in the context of those who hear it and see it demonstrated, but it must never be diluted so it becomes another Gospel.

Great stress has been laid recently upon the need for

'incarnational' mission. This combines the need for evangelism with the dimension of social concern, and many papers have been written on this subject in recent years. Churches all around the world need to rediscover the fact that evangelism and social transformation are actually two sides of the same coin. That such a discovery is possible is being shown by many of the younger churches in different parts of the world, where the reality of oppression and poverty, often created by exploitation by the powerful, are such enormous issues that Christians dare not remain silent, for to do so would be a negation of the Gospel itself. In the West, where individualism is so rampant, a necessary corrective comes from the two-thirds world where community is vital. These matters were of great concern to the writers of the New Testament, who explored the social implications of the Gospel upon the communities of God's people as well as the impact of the Gospel on the world at large.

The growth of giving to such agencies as TEAR Fund and Christian Aid gives testimony to a growing concern among Christians to be involved in caring for the physical, social and development needs of men and women. What must not be lost in such work is the spiritual motivation that provides the will and the nerve to be involved with people who are hurting and so be identified with them in their need. Such motivation must stem from a deep love for Christ that gives sacrificially of one's time, energy and resources, but which also will make use of every opportunity to speak of the One who inspires such love where this is possible or appropriate. As in the case of our Saviour who combined the demonstration of compassionate action to those in need with a proclamation of the Gospel, so it must be in his followers who seek to walk in his footsteps.

Instead of the barren argument as to whether evangelism is to be primary or not, Christians must be involved in loving and caring action on behalf of men and women in need. This will sometimes be the bridge to evangelism, sometimes the consequence of evangelism, but should always be a partner with evangelism.

Danger of Fads in Missions

Christians must beware of being so preoccupied with one aspect of mission that happens to be popular at a given period of time that other vital aspects are neglected or overlooked. Whilst it is commendable to see how many churches have become more conscious of a social dimension to the Christian faith, there is great need to maintain spiritual balance in not overlooking other, equally important, aspects of mission. All too frequently, for instance, Christians can alleviate their stricken consciences by giving money to hungry or sick people while overlooking equally valid types of ministry.

The phenomenal growth of the Church in Africa has caused a crisis because of the lack of biblically trained leadership. Projects to train elders and other lay leaders using Theological Education by Extension (TEE) struggle on with minimal funding. The development of facilities for higher theological education is seriously hampered by lack of adequate financial resources in many parts of the world. The Church in Africa may be growing, but the majority of its members are subsistence farmers seeking to eke out a precarious existence on the southern edge of the Sahara or Kalahari in drought conditions which defy description. Others live in countries where the inflation rate has gone through the roof. Several countries prohibit the sending of currency out of their borders, thus making transfer of funds from one country to another almost impossible, even where funds are available. Yet the Church desperately needs theologians, writers, pastors for urban churches who will be able to wrestle with the issues challenging the African churches from their own context. *Where are the financiers in the West who will underwrite such vital projects? Who will become partners with the growing churches of Africa and South America by releasing the resources entrusted to them by God for the work of his kingdom?*

Bible translation and literature work are also vital, providing the very foundations of the beginnings of the Church. However for tens of thousands of pastors of churches across the world the only books they have available may be a single copy of the New Testament or perhaps the whole Bible and a hymn book and perhaps one or two thin volumes in their own language. We urgently need, firstly to establish literature funds for some to be trained as writers, and secondly to establish publishing schemes for suitable books for each age group in the Church. In the English language there is such a superfluity of publications that it has become almost obscene by comparison with the poverty of printed material in the two-thirds world. It is recognised that there are no easy answers to such questions – but these questions demand answers. Our Lord's words still carry a serious warning to all to whom he spoke: 'Every one to whom much is given, of him will much be required' (Luke 12:48).

We do well to remember also the startling statistics that ninety per cent of the Christian workers serve ten per cent of the world's population, and the vast majority of missionaries still service existing churches. There is a continuing need to recruit, train and send missionaries who have that pioneer spirit to open up new areas where people have never heard the Gospel. They will have to be men and women who have a clear call from the Lord, whose faith is in the One who called them and not in themselves, who are willing to count the cost of sacrificial service in the difficult areas of the world.

How is It to be Achieved?

Sharing Resources

For some in the West, the best way to assist in this new development is by supporting key Christian national workers who otherwise would find it extremely difficult or impossible to fulfil their ministry. In some cases severe restrictions, or a total ban on the movement of currency out of a country, makes it virtually impossible for some nationals to get support for missionary work beyond their own borders.

Many young churches have a great need for *temporary* assistance for key projects in their countries that would be particularly difficult to finance initially. Some missions, deeply committed to long cherished principles of the indigenous church (i.e., self governing, self support, self propagation), have questioned the advisability of such support for national leaders. However, many are beginning to appreciate the dilemma which Christians in developing countries are facing. They have a clear mandate to work for their Lord, but sometimes the vision is not shared as yet by the churches with which they are associated. Here is where the financial resources of the Western churches can assist such leaders, provided that sufficient safeguards are made not to stifle local support, or to dictate the terms by which such leaders can operate, thus perpetuating a financial imperialism of the worst kind.

Such support schemes have worked in a number of denominational mission agencies for many years. Only recently have interdenominational mission societies begun to see the need for this type of assistance. Care must be taken not to think that this type of support replaces the need to send workers from Britain. It has a complementary role in giving support based on the scriptural basis of II

Corinthians 8:14: 'As a matter of equality, your abundance at the present time should supply their want.'

Co-operation

In recent years missionary societies in Britain have grown more aware that the task of mission in our world is too big for any one agency to achieve on its own. There is a greater willingness to learn from one another, and a growing commitment to share plans and personnel to meet such strategic opportunities.

Some societies have amalgamated where there seems to be little reason for the continued existence of two mission groups with almost identical principles and practices working in the same area. Some have shared their administrative headquarters allowing for the smaller societies to enjoy the use of more modern and sophisticated equipment while retaining their own identity. This has been true of the Whitefield House venture where BMMF International, Evangelical Union of South America and Regions Beyond Missionary Union share accommodation with the Evangelical Alliance, the Evangelical Missionary Alliance, Church Society, the Lausanne Committee for World Evangelisation and the Prison Christian Fellowship.

Sometimes churches plead to reduce the number of societies, especially when it comes to raising support for new projects or workers. However it must always be remembered that the variegated grace of God is seen in his multi-coloured, multi-gifted church. When the Lord has given a particular concern for a specialist ministry in literature, radio, relief, linguistics or transportation, who would dare to deny that he has prompted, called and chosen individuals or new teams to rise to the challenge? Sometimes it has been through a particular person who has been involved in one kind of ministry and who has been challenged by an apparently chance remark. For instance, Cameron Townsend was distributing Scriptures in the Spanish language in Guatemala when he heard the comment from one of the Indian population, 'If your God is so smart, why can't he speak our language?' Initially Townsend sought to encourage established mission groups to meet this need. In the end he began a new ministry under the name of Wycliffe Bible Translators. This team alone today numbers five thousand missionaries from all around the world.

Whatever the particular ministry that God has given, we need a commitment to one another, to learn from one another, and to share together the gifts and experience that the Lord has entrusted to each team. His work is never to be thought of as the preserve of one exclusive group, but for the good of the whole body. The main work of the Evangelical Missionary Alliance is to provide a forum where such sharing can take place, where mission executives can learn from one another and plan together. When joint action for missionary exhibitions or a youth missionary congress is required, co-ordination is vital.

Mobilisation of the Whole Church to Mission

The task of mission must not be restricted to specialist mission agencies. It is the responsibility of the whole Church. The tragedy of many churches today is that when mission is on the programme for a meeting the attendance drops. Those who stay away give the impression that mission is not their concern, or not their speciality. (Sometimes missionaries have been to blame because they have not been the best of communicators in their own culture when on home leave. An up-date on changing attitudes in the British culture is essential for all missionary personnel returning to their home country after an absence of three or four years.)

However, the task of mobilising and motivating congregations is the responsibility of the leadership of the churches. If there is regular exposition of Scripture from the pulpit, and systematic teaching of God's word that is faithful to the main biblical themes, then the subject of mission will feature prominently. Instruction programmes for different age groups and interest groups should include material that puts mission at the heart of the church's life rather than as an optional extra for those so inclined. The constant exposure of all Christians to what God is doing in the nation, in our continent and throughout the world will broaden the horizons of each Christian, encourage them to renewed effort and challenge them to make Christ known.

The use of creative ways to involve people in mission is essential. Recently a number of mission agencies have produced video programmes that can be used by different small groups in the church. Some of these are educational, others provide information for prayer.

Ministers, pastors and elders of local churches have the particular responsibility to:

a) **disseminate information.** Most leaders have a great deal of information sent to them through the mail, fed to them through magazines, journals and through the secular mass media. That material needs to be used and shared with each group in the congregation where it is appropriate.

b) **encourage interest.** This will only happen as the leader himself is interested in what God is doing around the world.

c) **impart instruction.** The teaching of Scripture is primary, but the careful instruction of believers in the doctrines, history and principles of the faith and of its outworking in our modern world will enable Christians to be firmly established in their faith and ready to share it with others. The local church is the seed bed for training for world mission.

d) **practise intercession.** The personal devotion to a ministry of prayer for the world will overflow in the public prayers in the congregation. When leaders fail to pray, it is likely that Christians whom they lead will also be prayerless.

e) **give inspiration.** This will only come as leaders themselves have found inspiration and vision in their Saviour and Lord. The opening of the heart and mind to God, to his word and to his world will enable them to inspire others.

f) **develop involvement.** Ultimately the measure of the success of a leader is seen in how those whom he has taught and led become involved in the mission of Christ in the world. Too often Christians are left to be spectators of what others are doing. Young people particularly will lose

interest unless they can become personally involved in projects, in work, in the ongoing plan of God.

Provision of Adequate Training

When the local church fails to equip a Christian for service and that Christian has a burning desire to serve his Lord, other ways must be found to provide adequate training. Most Bible and theological colleges can testify to the fact that all too often young Christians are inadequately grounded in the word of God and poorly equipped for Christian service. This then throws the weight of responsibility on the colleges. Where however a local church is giving a thorough training to its members, both in biblical instruction and practical training areas, the work of the colleges is then to concentrate on providing advanced training for cross-cultural ministry.

With the development of churches overseas, the requirement is for well-equipped workers to minister alongside their own national workers. Those involved in the training of such workers must be equipping those who are studying to be servants of Jesus Christ, who will *not* expect to be given leadership positions immediately on leaving college. The Lord Jesus called together a team to be his disciples, learners in his school. That pattern is one that should never change.

The training programmes that are devised will have to prepare men and women for patient and sacrificial service in a world that will be hostile and difficult to win. Therefore provision must be made for the discipline of a prayer life maintained at all costs, under the pressure of a study programme that at the time seems to be very full. This necessary grounding will be the backbone for future service where undreamt of pressures in language study, cultural adjustment and direct attacks from the kingdom of darkness are made on the new recruit.

But training must continue. Retraining programmes, upgrading courses, in-service refresher courses are necessary to keep abreast of changing situations or new developments. Many missionaries will change their assignment several times in their career. These changes need to be prepared for. This is particularly true for those thrust into leadership positions. Too many are given responsibility with little or inadequate management training. Missions must adequately plan for their younger workers to be prepared for greater responsibilities to seize these new opportunities. Such training can be found in different parts of the world; sometimes the help that is needed can be found in the university or secular training programmes as well as in the colleges that provide higher level training.

Prayer

It is necessary to remember that the mission of the church will encounter fierce opposition from the forces of the devil. He will not easily release those held in captivity, oppression or deprivation. The warfare in which Christians are involved seems to be more intense in certain countries than in others. However the opposition is just as effective when the cold, wet blanket of apathy and lethargy prevent any effective understanding of the Gospel as when an intense barrage of persecution is waged on would-be hearers of the word of life.

The commitment to a ministry of prayer by the churches is perhaps the most urgent call of all. Where a church fails to make prayer a priority in its own community, let alone for the world, then there is little hope of advance.

Why are there places in our world still without messengers of the Gospel? Is it not because Christians have failed to obey the command of Christ to pray the Lord of the Harvest that he will thrust out workers into his harvest field? Why do some missionaries return to their homeland broken, dispirited, discouraged? Is one reason that Christians have failed to uphold their missionaries in prayer?

The work of prayer is not glamorous; it is hidden, quiet and secret, but it is the vital ingredient for the progress of the Gospel throughout the world.

The task of missions is not over. The mission of the Church will continue until the end of the age. The mandate Christ gave to his Church before he returned to heaven after his resurrection has not been rescinded. We live in a different world to our forefathers. The task of mission needs to adapt to the changing times and situations of our modern world. But the Gospel is the same. It needs to be expressed in ways that will be understood by the different peoples of the earth. The Church in Britain needs to put mission back in the heart of the Church so that it may contribute its life and experience to those around the world who as yet have never heard of the good news of Jesus Christ.

Why Mission?

Martin Goldsmith

For the whole church to be involved in the active support of their mission, all the members must see mission world-wide as an integral part of biblical faith. It is possible that a missionary will be lovingly supported by those Christians who know him personally and therefore feel a bond of natural affection, but the rest of the church will probably take little interest.

There is growing doubt, even in biblically-based Christian circles, concerning the validity of active evangelistic mission in other countries. The reasons for this lie partly in a natural and right reaction to former imperialistic missionary approaches which seemed to be insensitive to other peoples and their faiths. But this has been compounded by a theological uncertainty concerning the uniqueness of Jesus Christ.

a) *The Natural Reaction*
God seemed to walk hand in hand with the British way of life. Good English manners and afternoon tea were surely vital ingredients of the Christian faith!

Today we Europeans have lost our self-confidence in the cultural disintegration of our societies during the last couple of decades. We now wonder whether we have anything to offer overseas. We realise that our cultures exhibit marked weaknesses, and yet it is impossible to wean our Christian Gospel away from our own backgrounds. Some Christians therefore begin to doubt whether it can be right for European believers to engage in mission.

Many also have a guilty conscience concerning the evils our forefathers inflicted on the peoples of Africa and Asia. While colonialism was not all bad, yet it is certainly true that we do have much of which we should repent. And sadly some missionary enterprises were closely linked to the colonialist authorities, so that many today feel that mission and imperialism are just two sides of the same coin. Instead of learning that modern mission must be humbly submitted to the indigenous church leaders, some have reacted by denying God's call to mission world-wide.

With such a guilty history, they ask, do we have the right still to go overseas to preach the Gospel of Christ?

The outworking of the Christian faith in the actual life of the British Church does not always inspire confidence. What right do we have to export our faith when it does not seem to work in our own country? In some churches we lack the demonstration of spiritual power, intimately loving fellowship and relevant vitality; in others arrogance, divisiveness and dogmatism may make it almost impossible to follow in Jesus' footsteps as suffering servants under the leadership of churches overseas. It is easy to be negative about the British Church and thus lose sight of our worldwide responsibilities. We shall not then be terribly interested in supporting our missionary brothers.

But such a negative view of the Church is unbalanced. While there is undoubtedly great need of God's work of reform and correction, yet we should not forget to give thanks for what God has graciously done for and in us. While the British churches abound in weaknesses, they also have some strengths which we should share with our brethren overseas.

b) *Theological Objections to Mission*

It is no longer fashionable either in secular philosophies or in theological thought to be dogmatic and assured of one's beliefs. This may be partly due to the influence of Eastern religions and the philosophy of existentialism. Certainly we live in an age when many are tolerant of tolerance, but definitely intolerant of any assured faith. If it is tacitly assumed that one cannot be sure of the unique truth of Jesus Christ of Nazareth, then people are unlikely to give their lives sacrificially for mission overseas or for the support of others in mission.

Theologically there are certain key questions which are

being debated today. They centre around the topics of revelation, salvation and judgement.

a) **Revelation.** It is noted that aspects of truth permeate the beliefs of other religions. We cannot deny, for example, the truth of monotheism in Islam even if we query some Muslim concepts of the character and workings of Allah. Where then does this truth come from? We cannot just say that it is due to the influence of the Jewish and Christian context in Mohammed's Arabia, for we also find aspects of truth in many tribal religions, Buddhism and Hinduism where there has been no Judaeo-Christian background. Theologians have talked about general revelation – the belief that God continues to reveal some aspects of himself through Nature and the conscience. God continues to work among non-Christians. Most would however emphasise that such general revelation does not lead to salvation, for this is still dependent on the more specific revelation of Jesus Christ.

It may also be said that truths in non-Christian religions are products of the original creation of man. The remnant image of God in man will lead to some truth in all his searchings after God.

In one way or another it seems sure that God's rule extends beyond the narrow confines of the Church and that he does reveal himself to some extent also to non-Christians.

b) **Salvation.** A sweeping and unfeeling condemnation of all who have not been evangelised horrifies many Christians today. Can God really be so callous? Is there no possibility of salvation for the sincere and godly non-Christian? Is the loving God really willing to damn the millions who have either never heard the Gospel or who have heard such an inadequate version of it that it is almost impossible for them to believe? Such questions move the hearts and minds of Christians today.

While most of us would want to affirm that all salvation is through Jesus Christ alone and depends totally on the efficacy of his cross and resurrection, yet some have moved beyond this. They may talk of a cosmic spirit of Christ who can work outside the Church among those of good will. It is the spirit of Christ which enlightens all men, they say with reference to John 1. This relates closely to earlier ideas first put forward by the Roman Catholic theologian Karl Rahner, who suggested that godly and upright non-Christians might in fact be 'anonymous Christians'. Although this concept has been largely rejected, yet the idea of salvation being available for non-Christians through the merit of Jesus Christ has remained strong. Inevitably this undermines the Christian's dedication to the task of mission.

c) **Judgement.** The supposedly Victorian emphasis on the horrors of Hell has backfired. In reaction against such negative preaching of judgement some have cut Hell right out of their theology and their preaching. Many nineteenth-century missionary pioneers (e.g. Hudson Taylor) were inspired to self-sacrificing missionary work by their vision of people being lost without Christ. The realities of sin and judgement – and they are realities – stood vividly before their eyes.

Motivation for mission should not rest entirely on the call to save men and women from judgement. We should also preach the Gospel because it is indeed joyfully good news. The positive delights of a living relationship with the Father through Christ and by the Spirit compel us to persuade all men to join us in the life of faith. We are also bound to engage in the missionary task because we long for the Lord we love to be honoured, worshipped and served as is his due. It grieves us to see his name ignored or dragged in the mud. So we are not only called to involvement in the missionary task because of the fearful reality of judgement for sin. But nevertheless this should be one aspect of our motivation.

It is not possible in this short chapter to deal seriously with these critical theological issues, but at least we must note here that they inevitably affect our missionary vision and thus also the degree of our missionary support.

Not Just Subjective

Why do some Christians give and pray with a selfless spirit of sacrifice in their support of overseas mission? What has pushed them to this?

Some mission leaders over the years have attempted to investigate what leads to people becoming keen supporters of their mission. It is generally agreed that people are more likely to get actively involved if they have met a missionary who has captured their interest or affection. Missionary societies therefore stress the importance of missionaries' personal contact with churches.

It may seem obvious that personal encounter stimulates support, but we have then to ask what role the Bible plays in motivating people. Christians affirm that the Bible is our ultimate authority in all matters of faith and practice. But when it comes to the matter of missionary vision and support, our participation depends on the subjective question of whether we have met a missionary who appeals to us. Of course it is true that missionaries, like all other Christians, are living epistles and ambassadors of Christ, so we expect God's word to come to us in and through them. But surely this subjective method of appeal should be secondary to fundamental biblical principles in the practice of our Christian life.

But sadly our normal teaching and preaching of the

Scriptures does not emphasise God's missionary vision for all nations and peoples.

Not Just Pride

'Our church supports seven different missionary societies'; 'we have sent six of our young people to other countries for mission work'; 'we have agreed as a church to give twenty per cent of our income to Christian work outside our own church'. Pride lurks threateningly behind even the best of our activities. All of us know the dangers of incipient pride both in our individual lives and also in our churches. While we rejoice in the missionary vision implicit in such quotations, we know that God looks on the heart rather than just on external works.

Smug self-satisfaction or boasting attitudes eventually stifle any vibrant spirituality. The pattern of the Bible and the 'suffering servant' example of Christ himself exalt meekness as the precondition for true life. Spirit-given fruitfulness depends on humility.

We dare not measure our Christian 'success' by the number of missionaries we support or how much we give to mission. The church is not a growth-conscious capitalist enterprise. Where motivated by status-seeking pride the church may flourish outwardly, but the Spirit may be quenched. And it is the Holy Spirit of life who calls people and thrusts them out into mission. It is the Spirit who softens our hearts so that 'the love of Christ can constrain us'. It is the Spirit who moves Christians to love their brothers working overseas and thus to support them by prayer, giving and loving care.

Not Just the Few

In many of our churches missionary concern has gripped the hearts of some members while others claim to have different interests. Even in churches where world-wide mission stands at the very heart of the church's life, in practice it tends to be just a few who really share that vision. Why is world-wide mission apparently a hobby of the few rather than an integral part of biblical Christianity for all Christians?

Is it because mission is often an extra activity which is not adequately integrated into the total life of the church? The missionary meeting or prayer group is additional to the regular programme of the church. The keen Christian, it is felt, *ought* to attend the Sunday services and the mid-week house Bible study, but a missionary meeting is considered quite optional. It is an unstated assumption that all Christians should be interested in worship and Bible study, but not all Christians will be interested in mission.

Or is it because there is a sharp divide between biblical teaching and mission? The two rarely seem to come together. Much of our Bible teaching is individualistic with little reference to God's world-wide vision for all nations and peoples. On the other hand many missionary meetings refer very little to the Bible – perhaps a text is given at the start of a talk, but then speakers often leave biblical teaching behind in order to concentrate on an account of their mission work overseas.

I vividly recall a Christian Union's pre-terminal conference which had invited another missionary and myself to be the speakers, but they had not thought of us as missionaries. They asked us to speak on particular sections of Scripture. The other speaker gave a series of superb addresses on the early chapters of Hebrews while I was asked to expound selected passages from Isaiah. The students had not expected missionary talks, but true exposition inevitably embraced the universal purposes of God. The vision and work of mission emerged naturally as part of the application and exposition. The students were deeply impressed and it changed their view of Scripture and of mission.

I have attempted elsewhere[1] to show that God's call to mission is not dependent on a few isolated passages – the Great Commission in Matthew 28; the first half of Romans 10; John 4:35; Acts 1:8. The whole Bible demonstrates God's concern for the whole world and all peoples. The Bible begins with the creation of the world and Adam, the father of all mankind. It concludes with 'the healing of the nations' (Rev. 22:2) and the prayer that 'the grace of the Lord Jesus be with all the saints' (Rev. 22:21). We note the plural 'nations' and the word 'all'.

If God's purposes embrace all peoples everywhere, his followers will naturally want to align themselves with his overall plan for the world. Some of us will be called to share the Gospel of Jesus Christ in one part of the world, others elsewhere. Some will share with one race of people, others with another. But God wants the good news of his love and salvation to be given to all peoples everywhere. And all of us will want to play a part in this great international vision of God. Even if we are not called to go to other countries or peoples, we shall gladly support God's work beyond our own borders.

But does God really want all peoples and races to follow Jesus Christ? This is one of the great questions of the New Testament. Previously it was assumed that Gentiles could only become followers of Jehovah by becoming like the Jews. They had to be circumcised and follow the Jewish Law of Moses, the Torah. In the New Testament the early Christians questioned whether it was allowable for Gentiles to become followers of the Jewish Messiah and the God of Israel. Much of the New Testament is written with this fundamental question in mind – is the Jewish Messiah only

---

[1] *Don't Just Stand There* (IVP, 1976)

for Jews and those who become Jews by circumcision? Or is the good news of Jesus also for Gentiles?

1. Luke/Acts

Although we have named Luke's second book the 'Acts of the Apostles', we might equally use the title 'Acts of the Holy Spirit'. The very first sentence of the book refers to the commandment which Jesus gave to his disciples, the apostles, through the Holy Spirit. Luke then goes on to talk of the gift of the Holy Spirit who would give them power for witness 'in Jerusalem, and in all Judaea and Samaria and to the end of the earth' (Acts 1:8). The Holy Spirit shares the missionary vision of the Father who so loved *the world* that he sent his Son for us all. The Spirit is the author of world-wide mission. When the Spirit gives power, men are moved to become witnesses 'to the end of the earth'. It is a contradiction in terms to say that one has been filled with the Spirit and yet does not have a deep concern for world-wide mission.

The early chapters of the Acts of the Apostles show the establishment of the Christian Church among Jews. Although the main action is centred on the holy city of Jerusalem, yet the message of Jesus the Messiah reaches out from there to Jews of all nations. At Pentecost the crowd consisted of devout Jews 'from every nation under heaven' (Acts 2:5).

As is so often the case in Scripture, the message of salvation comes in word and sign. The authority and reality of the preached message is backed up by the powerful works of the Spirit. Thus at Pentecost the miraculous sign of everyone hearing the message in their own language goes hand in hand with the preaching of Peter. Again, in Acts 3 the healing of a lame man immediately precedes an evangelistic sermon by Peter (3:12-26). This is of course a normal pattern in the Bible, not only in the Book of Acts.

The verbal promises of God in the various biblical covenants are always linked to visible signs – a rainbow, circumcision, baptism. In Matthew's Gospel the structure of the book gives long sections of teaching interspersed with a few chapters recounting the deeds and miracles of Jesus. Likewise in John's Gospel the author gives a variety of signs, each of which is followed by a preaching passage. Then finally the order is reversed. The final great word (John 13–17) is followed by the climactic deed of the death and resurrection of Jesus. The concept of 'word alone' is not really biblical.

The establishment of the Church in these early chapters of Acts is not only by word and sign, but also by the witness of the living community of the followers of Jesus. Luke underlines their powerful prayer together (e.g. 4:31), their unity in love (e.g. 4:32), their united worship in Temple and home (2:46), and their glad, joyful praise (2:46, 47). From this firm base in fellowship these early Christians were able to adventure out to their fellow Jews in evangelistic mission. Indeed we read in 1 John 1:3 that joyful, loving fellowship can be a motive for preaching. John says that he proclaims a message which he has himself seen and heard – but why? Because he longs 'that you may have fellowship with us'. When we enjoy a true Christ-centred fellowship of love and joy, we have confidence to preach the good news of Jesus Christ and we do so with a deep desire that others may join us in that fellowship. Our joy is not complete when we know lonely people are still outside that community of Christ. Likewise we know that other people cannot have full joy until they find it with us in the Father and the Son. So it is that 1 John 1:4 has the alternative reading 'that our/your joy may be complete'.

So the early mission of the Spirit establishes a firm base for the Church among Jews. The great question remains –

will the message of the Jewish Messiah reach out beyond Jewish circles? Is Jehovah for *all* peoples?

The Gentile Luke develops this theme. At the end of Acts 7 the stoning of Stephen is witnessed by the young Saul who was to become the great apostle to the Gentiles. Thus Luke prepares his readers for the conversion of Paul in Acts 9 and then the whole movement of the Spirit to Gentiles.

But between the Jewish chapters (1–7) and the conversion of Paul (9) Luke gives us a bridge between Jew and Gentile. Acts 8 recounts the working of the Spirit among the mixed Jew-Gentile race of the Samaritans. It then tells the story of the conversion of the Gentile Ethiopian eunuch who 'had come to Jerusalem to worship' (8:27).

In showing the Samaritans to be a bridge to the Gentiles, Luke was following the example of Jesus himself. Jesus prepared his disciples for wider mission beyond mere Jewish circles by frequent reference to Samaritans. He tells the shocking story of a Jew who is helped by a Samaritan – it would have been bad enough if the story had been of a Samaritan who was helped by a Jew! But it was almost unacceptable that a Jew might need to be helped by a despised Samaritan. He also heals ten lepers and we are told that only one came back to give thanks – and 'he was a Samaritan' (Luke 17:16). Then Jesus made a point of going through Samaritan villages on his way up to Jerusalem (Luke 9:51–56) and he reveals himself most particularly to a Samaritan woman (John 4). The Jews at that time tended to restrict the kingdom of God to pious male Jews. Jesus widens this idea of the kingdom by his loving relationship with this woman (note the emphasis on the word 'woman' in John 4) of Samaria who had had five husbands and was now living with a man who was 'not your husband' (John 4:18). By his emphasis on the Samaritans Jesus prepares his disciples for a wider future ministry which should also include Gentiles.

We notice in Acts 8 that the apostles have learned their lesson and so need no special call of God to go to the Samaritans. It is now so clear to them that the kingdom of the Messiah is also for Samaritans that Acts 8:5 simply records, 'Philip went down to a city of Samaria and proclaimed to them the Christ.'

The next step in the development of mission is to reach out to Gentiles. The apostles do not find that so easy. God needs to prepare Peter quite carefully. It is evident from the fact that Peter was staying in the house of a tanner that he had already been somewhat released from a rigid adherence to the Law, but still mission to unclean Gentiles was hard for him. God steps in therefore and gives him the horrifying vision of 'all kinds of animals and reptiles and birds' being let down on a sheet. 'Kill and eat,' is God's word to Peter. When Peter protests, God says, 'What God has cleansed you must not call common' (10:15). Only after this thrice-repeated word was Peter willing to receive the messengers of the Gentile Cornelius.

Paul too concentrates on the Jews alone until God forces him to include Gentiles in his mission. In Antioch of Pisidia Paul goes to the synagogue and preaches. By the next Sabbath wide-spread interest had grown in the town and 'almost the whole city gathered together to hear the word of God' (13:44). Soon Paul and Barnabas faced an embarrassing situation. The majority of the Jews began to revile Paul and contradict his message (13:45). But the Gentile crowds rejoiced in the free offer of eternal life and gloried in God's word (13:48). So Paul found himself almost compelled to warn the Jews that in rejecting God's word they were judging themselves 'unworthy of eternal life' (13:46). Then Paul reminded himself of God's prophetic word in Isaiah 49:6 and uttered those pivotal words for the whole history of the Christian church — 'we turn to the Gentiles' (13:46). Paul was indeed to be a 'light for the

Gentiles' to bring salvation 'to the uttermost parts of the earth' (13:47). The story of Acts unfolds with ever-widening mission to Gentiles, reaching even to Rome itself. 'This salvation of God has been sent to the Gentiles' (28:29).

The Gospel of Luke also begins in very Jewish fashion. The first three chapters have a strongly Jewish character (e.g. Luke 1:67–80), but already there are hints of wider Gentile mission. These chapters are like the overture of a symphony which already contains an introduction to the main themes which are to be developed later. So in Luke 1:33; 2:31/32; 3:6 we find a foreshadowing of the Gentile ministry of Jesus.

The bridge between the Jewish chapters and the wider Gentile ministry is the genealogy (3:23–38). In Matthew's Gospel the genealogy comes right at the outset of the book. It is a fitting introduction to the Jewish Gospel with its evidence of Jesus as the son of Abraham, the father of Israel. Luke's genealogy shows Jesus to be the son of Adam, the father of all men – and he notes that the father of the Gentiles is also the 'son of God' (3:38)! Luke's genealogy therefore comes fittingly as the bridge to the Gentile ministry which begins in chapter 4.

At the outset of his ministry Jesus reads the Scriptures in his home synagogue. He reads the message of Isaiah concerning social and spiritual liberty which he himself is sent to proclaim. But he cuts the reading short. He does not continue to read from Isaiah 61 how 'the day of vengeance of our God' will mean that aliens and foreigners will become slaves to Israel. In the Old Testament the salvation of Israel is often associated with the judgement of the Gentiles, but now Jesus changes that. The offer of salvation by grace through faith is open to all, Jews and Gentiles of all nations. After reading the Scriptures in the synagogue Jesus shows how even in the Old Testament

God's grace had reached out to Gentiles – to the widow of Zarephath, to Naaman the Syrian.

The same Jew–Gentile sequence is seen also in Luke 9 and 10. In Luke 9 Jesus sends out the twelve, the symbolic number for the people of Israel. In Luke 10 he then appointed seventy others also. Seventy was the traditional rabbinic number for the Gentiles, which accounts also for the choice of seventy elders to make the first translation of the Jewish Scriptures into a Gentile language (the Septuagint). Later however the rabbis debated whether perhaps the right number for the Gentiles was actually 72 – we need not go into the arguments in favour of this, but merely note here that later traditions replace the number 70 with 72 both in the number of elders who translated the Septuagint and also in Luke 10:1. The Jewish twelve are now completed by the addition of the Gentiles. As might be expected in Luke's writings, we have a Samaritan incident between the 12 and the 70 – namely Jesus going through the Samaritan villages en route for Jerusalem (Luke 9:51–56).

2. *Romans*

It is to be expected that Luke would emphasise in his writings that the Gospel is for all peoples. But what about Paul? In Ephesians he particularly stresses the equality and unity of Jew and Gentile. And in Romans he demonstrates that his calling to mission among Gentiles is a valid one. This was particularly needed because he wanted to use Rome as a launching pad for further Gentile mission to Spain.

In the very first sentence he notes that his apostleship has the aim of bringing all nations to the obedience of the faith (1:5). He then thanks God that the Romans' faith is proclaimed in all the world (1:8). And in these introductory verses he boldly affirms that he desires to reap a harvest among Gentiles and is indeed under obligation to all sorts of people (1:13/14). In this task his confidence is in the powerfully saving Gospel which is for 'everyone who has faith, to the Jew first and also to the Greek' (1:16).

He begins the presentation of his case by showing that all men, both Jews and Gentiles, have the identical problem of being under the power of sin. He first shows that Gentiles are sinners (1:18–32), then that apparently good people of whatever race ('whoever you are') are equally under condemnation and finally that Jews too are sinners (2:17–29). He sums up the argument in chapter three by stating that 'all men, both Jews and Greeks, are under the power of sin' (3:9) – and he underlines this by a string of proof texts (3:10–18).

Having proved the problem of sin to be universal for all nations and peoples, he now needs to demonstrate that the solution is equally universal in its availability. This he does at the end of chapter three. He shows how justification depends on the redemptive death of Christ. This justification is through faith, not by the works of the Jewish Law. If salvation came through the Jewish Torah, it would only be for Jews and those Gentiles who joined themselves to Israel by circumcision. But happily our salvation is through faith – and men of all races can have faith. The Gospel is therefore not just for Jews, but also for Gentiles from every race and continent.

Luther and the other reformers related Paul's argument to the problems of their own day. They were battling against a works-conscious Roman Catholicism. Paul was not fighting the same battle. He was struggling against a Jewish emphasis on the Torah as God's means of light and grace. So he shows that Abraham was justified by faith long before the Torah was given to Moses – but it should be noted that good works and merit were a possibility long before Moses' time! The argument is therefore not faith versus good works; it is faith versus Torah. And Paul fights this battle in order to show that mission to Gentiles is a necessary and right activity.

All this presents Paul with a problem. If Jews and Gentiles are equally under sin and are both offered justification by faith in the death and resurrection of Christ, what advantage has the Jew? Are God's covenants with Israel no longer worth anything? He looks for answers to this issue in chapters 9–11. The final answers come after much heart-searching in 11:11–36. The Jews have largely rejected the Gospel and this led to the opening of the door to Gentiles (see Acts 13 again). Paul trusts that the salvation of the Gentiles will lead to many Jews becoming jealous and wishing that they too could enjoy the beauty of life and love in Christ. And so a 'hardening has come upon part of Israel, until the fullness of the Gentiles come in, and so all Israel will be saved' (11:25/26). The sequence is then: a few Jews – many Gentiles – all Israel. Commentators abound in possible interpretations both of the words 'the fullness of the Gentiles' and 'all Israel', but I am convinced that at least it means a vast number both of Jews and Gentiles. Perhaps we might link this to God's great ultimate purpose that multitudes of people 'from every tribe and tongue and people and nation' (Rev. 5:9) should join together in the new song of praise and worship before the Lord Jesus.

It is in the context of God's universal mercies available for all that Paul then appeals to the Romans to present their bodies as living sacrifices (12:1/2). Surely also today God calls us equally to give ourselves unreservedly and sacrificially for the task of world-wide mission. We are to be his instruments in bringing his merciful life-giving salvation to Jew and Gentile, to people of all nations everywhere. Our question is not whether we should get involved. It is rather: how can I better serve the Lord and further his work of world-wide mission? We long that 'the Gentiles might glorify God for his mercy' (15:9) – and the Jews too!

3. John

It might be thought that the Gentile Luke and Paul, the apostle to the Gentiles, have an axe to grind in stressing that the Gospel of Jesus is for all nations everywhere. What then about John? While the limitations of space forbid much detailed exposition of John's Gospel, we must at least give an introduction – the reader can then privately study further.

The Prologue to the Gospel reminds us immediately of the creation story in Genesis, where God sets in motion the history of the whole world and all peoples. John therefore stresses 'the world', 'every man', 'all'. He contrasts the rejection of Jesus by 'his own people' with the open door for 'all' to become God's children. They are not adopted as children of God by natural blood-descent, but through divine rebirth (1:13). So it is that the lamb of God takes away the sin of the world (1:29).

R. Brown in his Anchor Bible commentary on John's Gospel demonstrates how the prologue introduces the theme of the whole book that Jesus is the perfect fulfilment of the Old Testament. He is the fulfilment of the creating word of God in Genesis, of the Temple festivals, of the Sabbath, of the manna in the wilderness, of the Temple itself etc.

The first twelve chapters prepare the way for the climactic fulfilment in the sacrificial death of Jesus. He is the ultimate sacrifice for sin and the unique way of salvation. As the 'I am', Jehovah himself, he can say that those who see or know him, see and know the Father. This saving knowledge of the Father depends on the reality of the cross and resurrection, the final 'sign' of John's Gospel.

John prepares the way for this final sign in the first twelve chapters. In this section the coming of the Greeks to Jesus is the climax (12:20ff.) The Old Testament did not normally expect Israel to go out in mission to the Gentiles, but expected that the communal life of the people of God would so reflect God's glory that the Gentiles would be drawn in to Zion like bees to honey. John sees the fulfilment of this in the Gentile Greeks coming in to Jesus – and this accounts for Jesus' apparently excessive reaction to the coming of the Greeks: 'The hour has come for the son of man to be glorified . . .' (12:23). Now he can move on to the cross through which he will 'draw all men to myself' (12:33). The way for mission to all nations everywhere is now prepared.

When the disciples meet with the risen Jesus (20:20) and their fear (20:19) is turned to gladness (20:20) and peace (20:19, 21, 26), Jesus breathes on them. He tells them to 'receive the Holy Spirit' (20:22) and sends them out in mission. 'As the Father has sent me, even so I send you' (20:21). What an all-embracing commission!

Our mission to the world is no narrow task. It will involve us in passing on the evangelistic message of Jesus' salvation – and there are still multitudes of people in every country who have never heard the Gospel or who know very little of what Jesus has done for them. Pioneer evangelism is still badly needed in every continent. But mission is not only evangelism. It *is* evangelism, but it will also include Bible teaching, training and other ministries within and under the leadership of existing national churches. In this way we shall help them to reflect God's glory more fully in their life as the people of God; and we shall also help them to fulfil their evangelistic mission both locally and internationally.

How did the Father send the Son? Perhaps the key New Testament understanding of the mission of Jesus is found in the 'suffering servant' concept. Jesus came to serve and thus to give his life (Mark 10:45). If we are to be sent in like manner, we must be willing to give all for the sake of others. Our calling is to serve a needy world in all its spiritual, social, psychological, physical, economic, political needs.

As disciples of Jesus Christ all of us are sent into the world to serve, whatever the sufferings this may lead us into. Some of us will be called to the world in our own street, village or town. Others will be called further afield – this is just a geographical detail. But all of us will share the biblical vision of a Gospel for all nations and peoples everywhere. And we shall demonstrate this international vision either by going to serve other peoples or by loving, serving support of our brothers and sisters who are personally engaged in mission among other peoples and in other lands. We work together with Christ and with each other towards that great goal when 'the earth will be filled with the knowledge of the glory of the Lord' (Habakkuk 2:14) and when the redeemed 'from every tribe and tongue and people and nation' will join the heavenly worship 'to him who sits upon the throne and to the Lamb' (Rev. 5:9, 13). What a privilege we have!

About the Authors

Martin and Elizabeth Goldsmith joined the Overseas Missionary Fellowship in 1960 and were married in 1962. They served in North Sumatra and then Singapore, returning to the UK in 1971, when Martin joined the staff of All Nations Christian College, Ware, Herts. In 1973 Elizabeth also joined the staff. They have three children. Elizabeth is author of *God Can be Trusted* and *Going Places* and Martin has written several books including *Don't Just Stand There* and *Islam and Christian Witness*.

John Wallis. 'Without a period as a missionary in South Korea, I could never do my present job,' says the British Director for Overseas Missionary Fellowship. Married with three children, John was formerly in the Anglican ministry and still keeps his hand in as Honorary Curate at St Nicholas Parish Church, Sevenoaks, where he lives. His work takes him to East Asia every three years and to Europe frequently, as well as all over Britain. He is editor of *We Believe in Mission*.

Anne Townsend worked as a missionary doctor in Thailand for sixteen years with the Overseas Missionary Fellowship. Her husband, John, is a surgeon. They returned to the UK in 1980 to make a home for their teenage children. Since then Anne has been full-time editor of *Family* magazine. In 1985 she takes up a new job as Director of CARE Trust. She is author of twelve books including *Missionary Without Pretending*, *Prayer Without Pretending* and *Time for Change*.

Stanley Davies is the General Secretary of the Evangelical Missionary Alliance, a post he took up in September 1983. Prior to that he was Director of Missions at Moorlands Bible College, Dorset, for a three-year period. With his wife Margaret and his family he spent fifteen years as a missionary in Kenya serving with the Africa Inland Mission in church related ministries and theological education. He was trained as a surveyor and travelled widely in Africa and western Asia before entering missionary service.

For Further Reading

The Eleventh Commandment (IVP) Peter Cotterell
Move Out (STL/MARC Europe) Michael Duncan
(publishing December 1984)
Going Places (IVP/STL Books) Elizabeth Goldsmith
Don't Just Stand There (IVP/STL Books)
Martin Goldsmith
Get Your Church Involved in Mission (OMF Books)
Michael Griffiths
Ten Sending Churches (MARC Europe/EMA) Edited by
Michael Griffiths (publishing Autumn 1984)
What on Earth are You Doing? (IVP) Michael Griffiths
Operation World (STL Books) Patrick Johnstone
The Christian at Work Overseas (TEAR Fund) Edited by
Ian Prior
Turning the Church Inside Out (BMMF International)
H. Rowdon
Christian Mission in the Modern World (Falcon)
John R. W. Stott
Today's Tentmakers (Tyndale) J. Christie Wilson

MICHAEL GRIFFITHS
Ten Sending Churches

Ten ministers from different areas and different denominations describe how their church has become actively involved in mission.

Mission is a sadly neglected field today. Too many churches are consumed with their own problems to appreciate the link between mission, evangelism and a living and growing Christian fellowship. What is needed is a series of models: churches which have seen the importance of mission and have responded to the need for committed and prayerful support.

There is no single 'right' way of backing mission. Here, however, are imaginative approaches which will provide real examples of how your church can participate in the spreading of the Gospel.

Michael Griffiths is Principal of London Bible College and Consulting Director of the Overseas Missionary Fellowship.